W9-AAD-156

OX HERDING IN WISCONSIN

OX HERDING IN WISCONSIN

Richard Quinney

Borderland Books

Copyright ©2013 Richard Quinney. All rights reserved. No part of this book may be reproduced in any form without written permission from the publisher, with the exception of brief excerpts for review purposes.

Published by Borderland Books, Madison, WI
www.borderlandbooks.net

Publisher's Cataloging-In-Publication Data
Quinney, Richard.
   Ox herding in Wisconsin / Richard Quinney.— 1st ed.
   Includes bibliographical references and index.
   ISBN: 978-0-9835174-2-9

   1. Enlightenment (Buddhism) 2. Religious life—Zen Buddhism. 3. Herding—Wisconsin. 4. Quinney, Richard. 5. Allegories. I. Title.
BQ4398 .Q554 2013
294.3/442   2012911252

Printed in the United States of America
First edition
Designed by Ken Crocker
Printed by Worzalla Printing
Typeset in Sabon

Cover illustration by Carol Chase Bjerke

The Buddha is just an old monk in the Western Heaven—
Is that something to look so hard for day and night?
It's you who are the Buddha, but you just won't see—
Why go riding on an ox to search for an ox?

—Wuxue Zuyuan (1226–1286)

Contents

Preface

This is a daybook inspired by the parable of ox herding. For a long time writers and artists and students of Buddhism have found spiritual guidance in the herding of the ox. The material world may be an illusion, with much of human suffering caused by desire and attachment, but understanding and enlightenment are possible in our daily lives. In the course of a year, I have considered carefully the living of my life.

The paradox of ox herding is that the ox from the beginning was never missing. The ox was there all the time, within the seeker. The ox and the seeker are one, from beginning to end. Enlightenment is the realization of this truth.

Ox herding offers instruction on how we might live—not that we will suddenly reach the final stage of enlightenment as a permanent state of being. What we may experience is a momentary revelation in one stage or another, at any given moment. There are days when we may go through several of the stages of ox herding, only to return to the beginning of the search. But the awareness of the possibility of even brief moments of enlightenment is now basic to the living of a life. With attention and practice, ordinary life is a journey toward awareness, understanding, and enlightenment. The ox you are searching for is your own true self.

Autumn

1. The Truest Sentence That You Know

Won't you come along with me as this autumn season begins? I have something to tell you. I think of Ernest Hemingway, of nearly a century ago, squeezing the peel of little oranges into the edge of the flame, waiting for the words to come. He walks to the window, looks over the roofs of Paris, and thinks to himself: "All you have to do is write one true sentence. Write the truest sentence that you know." He then wrote the stories of things he knew. Late in life he would tell us that writing stories when he was young in Paris was good and severe discipline.

I know the writing that is good and severe discipline. Many times writing has been for me about the only discipline I had or needed, and it was good. In the telling of the story—in the writing—I have been able to consider carefully what I am experiencing in my life. Writing is a way to understand the experience, to learn from it, and a way to go on.

Now, late in my seventies, much of what I am experiencing in my daily life is connected to aging. The physical signs are increasingly evident. I know that my condition is shared by all others of my age, past and present. Mortality is of grave concern. Begin with the truest sentence that you know.

2. Mindfulness

I write in this journal to grasp the present moment. The mind of the one who writes may be open and receptive, floating above the empty page. And what comes to mind may be a thought about something that happened a long time ago. When I place myself in the aura of that past, I do so in the awareness of my present time.

Words by Buddhist monk Achaan Chah have brought me to attention many times before, and serve now as an inspiration and guide throughout this book.

> Try to be mindful and let things take their natural course. Then your mind will become still in any surroundings, like a clear forest pool. All kinds of wonderful rare animals will come to drink at the pool, and you will clearly see the nature of all things. You will see many strange and wonderful things come and go, but you will be still. This is the happiness of the Buddha.

Writing in this journal is my meditation and my repose.

The Willow

3. A Classic Tale

It is late autumn of 2010 in this city in the midst of lakes, in a house on a hillside. My home is of classical proportion, my Ithaca of Homer's classical tale of Odysseus. In the morning, I may rise to the rose-red fingers of the dawn and imagine myself as Telemachus, son of Odysseus, and step from my bedroom, handsome as a god.

But today I will not rise with such mythical splendor. Mist and fog are outside my door, and rain is in the forecast for the day. I feel more like the father, Odysseus, returning from the long voyage over the sea. I am not alone, of course, and share my fate with other wanderers of my age. A friend wrote to me during the night of feeling the effects of growing older. In the morning mail is a letter, with the salutation: "We're growing older, my friend." I welcome his warm wishes.

Midway in his voyage away from home, Odysseus travels to the underworld, to the land of the dead, to consult the prophet Tiresias. There, Odysseus sees what it means to be dead and loses any illusions that death might be better than life. The eventual death of Odysseus is foretold by Tiresias.

The voyage of many years by Odysseus comes to an end. When he returns home, his true identity is revealed to his waiting wife, Penelope. In resignation and acceptance, he tells Penelope of the prophecy: "All this, the prophet said, will come to pass." This said, Odysseus and Penelope confide in each other and rejoice in reunion. Homer, the chronicler of the classical tale, gives us these fine words:

Rejoicing in each other, they returned to their bed,
The old familiar place they loved so well.

In the here and now. In the world of the living. Far from the prophet and the prophecy in the underworld. For the time being, the prophecy of imminent death can be ignored. The gift of life is all that matters now.

4. Good Fortune

When I get older. I will quote a line from a poem that uses the word when in the first sentence, from *No Beginning, No End,* by Zen master Jakusho Kwong. He has just recited a line from a ninth-century poem by Tozan-zenji:

> When you understand self which includes everything,
> You have your true way.

Kwong explains: "This *when* at the beginning of these lines marks the exact point in time and space where the awareness of this original mind manifests into wisdom and compassion. It's like the sound of my stick striking against the floor: *When!* That's the moment of your realization, and this realization is the entirety of Zen, revealing yourself and helping the many because they are also you." The *when* is right now, this moment, when I am aware that I have arrived at getting older.

For the record, nearing the end of the year, my aging has brought me to these matters of health: chronic lymphocytic leukemia that is treated regularly with chemotherapy; arthritis that has destroyed most of the cartilage in my right hip, likely requiring hip replacement; high blood pressure that is now controlled by medication; a brain hemorrhage six years ago that continues to be monitored; always the enlarged prostate that is treated with medication; high cholesterol that is lowered with the taking of statins; occasional treatment for small areas of skin cancer; and susceptibility to infections because of lowered immune system. Built into the aging process are the natural deteriorations and diseases of the body and the mind. All this, the prophet said, will come to pass. I am thankful for the life that I have, and I think of myself as being a fortunate man. I imagine myself as being Odysseus returning from a long voyage.

5. The Photographer's Life

Late in his life, photographer Harry Callahan would go to the park in Atlanta, where he had moved, to make photographs. Near his home, he would venture out and occasionally point his camera into the trees. In 1992, seven years before he died, he told an interviewer, "I always see people around here jogging, and I know if I had to go a block I don't think I could do it." His life was different now, he noted, but he still wanted to photograph, and wished his work to reflect this stage of his life. As throughout his life, Callahan had the desire to do something that would benefit humanity, and making photographs was central to his spiritual life. He told the interviewer, "So far I still look forward to going out and photographing."

The last photograph made by Edward Weston likewise inspires me. Photographing in his later years was as important to Weston as it had been throughout his earlier life. The final years in Carmel were documented in an exhibition at the Art Institute of Chicago, which I made certain to see several years ago.

In 1945 Weston began to experience the first symptoms of Parkinson's disease. Gradually he lost his strength and ability to photograph. He took his last photograph in 1948, a short distance from his hillside house overlooking the Pacific. His son Cole often helped him negotiate the cliffs and slippery tide pools, lugging the heavy view camera and tripod over the boulders.

The last photograph that Weston made was of rocks scattered on a beach at Point Lobos. The assistant who was with him that day later said that there was little in the scene to signal a distinguished photograph, but that Weston saw on the beach the physical results of forces spent. Later David Travis wrote of this last photograph: "At the age of sixty-two, in this seemingly non-descript photograph, Weston had come to know the meaning of capturing what seemed like nothing to everyone else. Although his health had failed him, his imagination had not."

During his last years of photographing, Travis writes, "Weston had come to see life not just as the exhilaration of a moment, but as a complicated cycle replete with mysteries and resolutions." And when Weston was no longer able to take photographs, to climb rocks and walk the beach at Point Lobos, he worked in his studio, overseeing the printing of the images that he had made during the course of his life.

6. Journeys at Home

The world one travels in becomes smaller as the traveler ages. Even daily, the amount of time spent out of doors decreases, limited, certainly, during these weeks and months that motion is reduced by arthritis of spine, hips, and knees. My principal navigation is from floor to floor and room to room. I take new inspiration from the eighteenth-century French writer Xavier de Maistre, who told of his walks in his bedroom in *A Journey around My Room*. Later he would tell of his travels to the window, looking into the night sky, in *A Nocturnal Expedition around My Room*. He was making discoveries in his daily life that had escaped him in former travels. In the foreword to a recent translation of de Maistre's work, Alain de Botton made this elegant observation about de Maistre's journeys at home: "De Maistre's work springs from a profound and suggestive insight: that the pleasure we derive from journeys is perhaps dependent more on the mindset with which we travel than on the destination we travel to." A newfound awareness of the sights and sounds of daily activities may come when the physical distance that one travels is diminished. In loss there can be something gained.

7. A Prophecy

Do we need a prophet to tell us what surely will come to pass? Maybe it is the authority and the urgency of the voice of prophecy that helps us accept the inevitable. And especially if that voice is grounded in religious tradition, if the prophecy is of divine providence. An act of the gods. "What ought to be, shall be," the prophets proclaim, and we are comforted.

Prophecy may come to us in the mythic world of the classics. Odysseus meets the blind prophet Tiresias while exploring the underworld. Prophecy is inherent to the Judeo-Christian tradition, our being moving in the direction of what is demanded. The proclamations of the prophets are severe. Amos proclaims: "Let judgment roll down like waters, and righteousness like a mighty stream." Faith and belief sometimes divert the sting of death.

Or let that prophecy be found in the natural history of the world. We are creatures in a world filled with its own wonders and mysteries. The facts themselves— the facts that we have determined through imagination—are amazing to behold. We humans, among all the creations, are an intimate and integral part of the ever-evolving universe. Although not certain of purpose, we know that we are not alone.

It takes a lot of courage—nevertheless—to be human. We know what is coming and what is to pass. All the prophets, sacred and secular, tell us what we can expect, for certain. For a long time, we walk on a tight wire, balancing between acceptance of the prophecy and denial of the prophecy. Along the way, at various times and in different ways, we find some resolution. Is not my daily time in this room filled with contemplation and the possibility of resolution? I'll begin with a meditation at the start of my travels each day.

8. Cows at the Farm

When you grow up on a dairy farm, on a farm of 160 acres in southern Wisconsin, much of your life is tethered to the barn. In the barn were the cows, the Jerseys and Holsteins that were milked twice each day. At one end of the barn were the stalls filled with calves. At the other end, pacing back and forth in the pen, watching us each morning and night, was the great bull. The chores, their patterns and rhythms, changed during the seasons of the year. The path between the house and the barn was well worn. That path has stayed with me for the whole of my life, no matter how far I traveled from the farm.

During the cold days of winter, as icicles grew longer along the eaves of the barn, the cows were let out of the barn to gaze into the sun and to linger in the barnyard. Always on the winter mornings, my father and we two sons would rise early, dress warmly, and make our way to the barn, often through the fresh snow that had come during the night. The cows would get up from their stalls, breathing and filling the barn with musty air. We would turn on the radio for early morning music and news. Cats, lazy after a night's sleep, would emerge from their beds under the straw. The bull in the heavily barred stall at the far end of the barn would bellow a morning greeting. Strapping the milking machines to the cows, placing the cold milk cups to udders, and turning the valves above the stanchions, we began the morning milking. On the mornings when the electricity had gone out because of a storm, we would sit on our wooden milk stools, placing our heads against the cows' bodies, and milk by hand the herd of cows.

With spring came the birthing of farm animals. Nightly trips were made to the pig house to care for the sows and to watch for the birth of new litters. The lambs were born with ease, sometimes in the snow, occasionally with the surprise of twins. The birth of calves received special attention, due to the economic importance of new stock and the potential problems of giving birth. The veterinarian would make several trips to the farm in advance of the births. Extraordinary procedures would be required when hooves were pointed in the wrong direction and the calf had to be pulled out of the mother. Late in the spring I would select a calf to feed, nurture, and groom for a project that would take the growing calf, now a heifer, to the county fair at the end of summer.

Our veterinarian had come from Colorado to Wisconsin to practice his profession. He retained his western ways and gave me a lariat, a rope made of the finest sisal and a brass honda braided into the end. Still a valued possession, the lariat hangs on a hook high above my desk. He taught me how to use the lariat, how to swing it in a wide loop to land around the neck of a calf or cow. On summer evenings, I took great pleasure riding my horse to the far end of the pasture, east of the barn, to round up the cows, bringing them back to the barn for the evening milking. I had become the herder of cows. The meaning of this, the metaphysical and spiritual ramifications, would only grow as the years passed and I became older.

9. Evening Prayer

Lately I have thought about the evening prayer that I would recite each night as a child when my mother put me to bed. I have had passing thoughts over the years that the prospect of death was not a proper subject for a tender child as the lights were turned off and he was left alone until time to rise and go to the barn with his father and brother for another milking of the cows. But I am beginning to realize that the content of the evening prayer of my childhood, a Puritan prayer recorded in *The New England Primer*, has provided me with a spiritual center for my life. And, at this time in my life, the prayer is becoming important for the preparations I must make.

> Now I lay me down to sleep;
> I pray the Lord my soul to keep;
> If I should die before I wake,
> I pray the Lord my soul to take.

After childhood, I ceased to say an evening prayer. No petitions were made, no praises were uttered, and no words of thanks were spoken in prayer. I might have sensed the need for prayer, but to what or to whom would I be praying? The image of a deity, a god, once available to the child, had vanished. Other notions of the infinite and the eternal, however vague, had replaced God. And what once was prayer was becoming a sustained sense of wonder beyond words.

In years of meditation, I have attended to the unknown and the unfathomable with a quieting of the mind, contemplation, speculation, and often a letting go of thought and desire. All the while, I have been thankful for life, and thankful for the real people in my life, for friends, colleagues, and family. My world—and my well-being in that world—has been shaped by the attention I have given to my spiritual life. With renewed intention, I may know my efforts by the name of prayer.

10. Ox Herding

The herding of cattle—and the stories of the herding of cattle—began long ago. The cow played an important part in emerging agriculture and was revered as a sacred animal. When attempts were made to give spiritual guidance to daily living, it was to the image of the cow that Hindu storytellers and Buddhist monks turned. Gradually, over a period of at least a thousand years, the parable of ox herding developed, with images and poems and commentaries known today in several versions.

The ox herding story is a guide for gaining enlightenment, a way to discover our true nature. The material world may be an illusion, with much of human suffering caused by desire and attachment to the illusory world, but understanding and enlightenment are possible in the living of our daily lives. The classic story of ox herding tells of ten stages in the course of enlightenment:

One Searching for the Ox. The oxherd has lost the ox. He is separated from his true self, the Buddha nature within. He begins searching for what is already there.

Two Seeing the Tracks. With the help of stories and teachings and sacred texts, the oxherd finds the first traces of the ox.

Ox Herding at the Farm

Three Seeing the Ox. The oxherd catches a glimpse of the ox. It is only the backside, the heels and the tail, but it is enough to convince the boy that there is an ox and that he has seen it.

Four Catching the Ox. The ox is found at the end of the field. The struggle to catch the ox begins. Effort is required.

Five Taming the Ox. The oxherd keeps a firm hold on the rope as he takes the ox along the path through the pasture.

Six Riding Home on the Ox. The struggle is over; the oxherd no longer fears losing the ox. With ease the boy rides the ox home.

Seven The Ox Forgotten, the Self Alone. The ox has disappeared because the enlightened oxherd is home and no longer needs the ox. The oxherd realizes that the ox is within the one who has been seeking.

Eight The Ox and the Self Forgotten. Vanished are both the ox and the oxherd. Equanimity prevails. Even the search for the sacred has ended.

Nine Returning to the Source. No need to strive. All things change, and nothing remains the same.

Ten Entering the Marketplace with Helping Hands. Life is in the ordinary living of life—with compassion toward all beings.

Home, home on the range. Where the deer and the antelope play. Where seldom is heard a discouraging word, and the skies are not cloudy all day. On road or range you are finally homeward bound. With good fortune, and attention and practice, your ordinary life is a journey toward awareness, understanding, and enlightenment. Your true nature was present from the beginning. The ox you have been searching for, and riding, is your own self, which someday might be known.

11. Our True Nature

Not so long ago, when the end of life seemed nearer than usual, I asked a Zen teacher for a thought that might help me in this time of need. Essentially, he said, we live our lives with an illusion, an illusion that we know what life is. What is there to lose, then, but our illusion? If we don't know what life is, how can we know about death? Perhaps death is the end of the illusion. No birth, no death—Zen masters have said.

How are we to live if we cannot know the meaning of life? Desiring to know the meaning of life and death, when the knowing is not humanly possible, causes further suffering. How then to live, how to release ourselves from the attachment to the impossible questions? As long as I can remember, from the time I would herd cows back to the barn for another milking, I have searched for the meaning of life and for guidance on how to live my life.

The allegory of ox herding offers instruction on how we might live—not that we will suddenly reach the final stage of enlightenment as a permanent state of being. What I have experienced is a momentary revelation in one stage or another, at any given moment. There are days when I go through all of the stages of ox herding, only to return to the search at the beginning. But the awareness of the possibility of even brief moments of enlightenment, through attention and action, is now basic to the living of my life.

The seeker must seek; such is the life of the pilgrim. And this is the core of the existential problem. For the seeker cannot know what is being looked for until it is found. The paradox of ox herding is that the ox from the beginning was never missing. The ox was there all the time, within the seeker. The ox and the seeker are one, from beginning to end. As the Zen master Wuxue Zuyuan wrote in the thirteenth century:

It's you who are the Buddha, but you just won't see—
Why go riding on an ox to search for an ox?

The ox that is being sought, the ox that is to be tamed, is one's self. And in the end, an end that can be arrived at daily, the seeker returns to the world of everyday life. At that time, both ox and seeker are forgotten. Such is liberation.

12. Love among the Ruins

Is not the past a sort of ruin? Certainly, the past is an eternity, as Henry David Thoreau envisioned it, just as the future is an eternity—a time everlasting, but inevitably outside the concrete reality of the present. Yet, the remembered past is part of our present reality, and the imagined future shapes our living of the present. Both past and future are ruins in that they are without the substantive reality of the present moment.

The past, as it recedes in time and imagination, disintegrates and falls apart. A weathering takes place, a dilapidation and decay of what once was. All traces of the past may vanish. Or if something remains, something physical or remembered, it is a skeleton of its former self but a vivid remnant that retains its hold on the present. A ghost, welcome or unwelcome, to those who are living now.

I have discovered once again, after an absence of some years, the painting by Edward Burne-Jones titled *Love among the Ruins*. Originally a gouache painted in the early 1870s, it was damaged a few years later in an attempt to photograph it. Burne-Jones immediately made an oil painting of the same subject, which hangs today in the great parlor of a manor house in England.

The painting was inspired by Robert Browning's poem "Love among the Ruins" (1852). In a meditation on the contrast between past and present, the speaker is in a meadow where sheep are grazing among the ruins of a great city. Armies once marched here, battles were fought, and towers stood tall where now there is a single turret. A girl waits, looking at the same place where a king once looked over a city. Nothing is left of what was fought for, and there is nothing to show for the blood that was shed. All has returned to the earth. The poet prefers the grass and the love between the two lovers now meeting among the ruins. Browning ends his poem with these lines:

> With their triumphs and their glories and the rest!
> Love is best.

The past is a source of the melancholy and beauty that give depth to our lives in the present. The past adds dimension, a necessary depth, to our daily lives. Life—perhaps at its fullest—is love among the ruins.

13. The Natural World

My spiritual path, even during my early childhood years, has been in the natural world. The devotion may be a product of a Methodist upbringing, but my sense of the divine has always been grounded in nature. And nature—as the basis of a religious faith—is filled with infinite possibilities. The world of nature is more than we can ever humanly fathom.

Being a naturalist requires a faith that is shared by all religions. One assumes—has faith—that the human mind can understand the natural world. The quantum physicist posits that everything is also something else. Energy, according to such thinking, becomes matter and matter becomes energy, or maybe both at the same time, depending upon your ways of observation. Thus, we living beings are matter today, and we return to energy as the matter of the body decays with death. Nothing is lost in the universe. The atoms that were made at the creation of the universe are the same atoms that are in the universe today. The same atoms and the same number of atoms. But little is known about the great portion of the universe that is beyond observation. There is scientific speculation on the existence of something conceived of as dark matter.

Much of nature is beyond human observation, just as religious faith is beyond what can be known. Nature, if certainty is desired, is not a substitute for religion. Nature has its own mystery and inability to be known. You could find all the religion necessary in your life by walking through woods or looking into the evening sky, or venturing into the marsh below the farm when you were very young. There is a world of religion outside the theism of any theology.

A Zen teacher reminded me that we all inhabit an illusionary world. Our minds—as evolved—perceive a reality that is a function of the human brain. Our minds imagine a reality, metaphorically, of mice living inside a grand piano. A mouse in a grand piano will never be able to see a world outside the confines of the piano.

What we know, what we think we know, is within the boundary of the mind. And, equally, what we believe is bounded by our capacity to believe. Science and religion, necessarily, are both matters of faith. Both give us the illusions by which we live our lives. How precious this life—and how in need we are for the compassion that we give one another.

14. The Earth Will Remember Us

A long time ago, when living in New York, I recited these lines from a poem by Swedish writer Pär Lagerkvist to my eleven-year-old daughter Laura as we held hands crossing the street:

> One day you will be one of those who lived long ago.
> The earth will remember you just as it remembers the
>   grass and the woods,
> the rotting leaves.
> Just as the soil remembers
> and just as the mountains remember the winds.
> Your peace shall be as unending as the sea.

Laura expressed interest but said with some humor in her voice that she did not find the words very reassuring. Only later, much later, in one's life could these lines of poetry give some comfort, maybe a great deal of comfort.

I have placed three of my nature photographs in a single frame to form a triptych. On the left is the marsh at the farm; in the center is the bur oak in the middle of the pasture east of the barn at the farm; and on the right is a landscape of bedrock and trees at the Jens Jensen children's park near my house. I call my construction "Wisconsin Altarpiece."

The inspiration for my altarpiece is a painting for an altarpiece by the nineteenth-century artist Caspar David Friedrich. Titled *The Cross in the Mountains* (1808), it was controversial in its time, causing a public scandal because of its unusual treatment of a classic religious theme. Depicted in the painting is a carved and gilded crucifix on the summit of a mountain, with rays of the setting sun radiating into the encroaching night sky. Friedrich originally thought that the painting and accompanying frame would serve as an altar at Tetschen Castle, in Bohemia. Today it hangs in a museum in Dresden, the resting place of a work of religious imagery within the secular and natural world of nature. Nature is celebrated in what continues to be called the Tetschen Altarpiece, and the crucifixion is an artifact in the landscape. God has all but disappeared in a scene that depicts the wonder of nature. As in Lagerkvist's poem, the Earth will remember us.

15. Resurrection Symphony

I am listening to Gustav Mahler's Second Symphony, the Resurrection Symphony. In the fourth movement, the mezzo-soprano sings:

> I am of God and will return to God!
> Dear God will give me a little lamp,
> will light me on to eternally blessed life!

In the fifth movement, the chorus and soprano soloist sing:

> O believe!
> You were not born for nothing,
> have not lived and suffered in vain!

The chorus and mezzo-soprano respond:

> What is created must perish!
> What dies must be reborn!
> Leave off trembling!
> Prepare yourself to live!

Nothing is lost. Such is the promise of the sounds from a great symphony.

16. Memory Stronger Than Time

There is spiritual truth in the line that Merle Haggard repeats in his song "My Favorite Memory": "I guess everything does change except what you choose to recall." In a sense, in the mind and soul of the beholder, a memory seemingly stops time, holding you in the moment of what once was. Certainly your vivid memory has a reality of its own. Time no longer is of the essence.

The man who served as an inspiration and guide for most of my adult life, Marshall Clinard, died this past summer. He lived a long and adventurous life, to the age of ninety-eight. He spent last winter on Sanibel Island in a house he had recently purchased. Returning to the high altitude of Santa Fe with some difficulty, he lived through the spring months into the early days of summer. He had invited me to visit him on the island during the winter, but I had been detained by matters of my own health.

Marshall, as professor of sociology and mentor, followed with interest and concern the lives and academic careers of his former students. Wherever I turned, Marshall was nearby, sometimes in bewilderment, but always in support. Whenever one of his students published a new book, Marshall was certain to follow with a letter of acknowledgment and a critique of the book.

Two weeks before he died, he sent me a full-page letter telling me what he found of interest in my recently
published book *A Lifetime Burning*. Marshall is an intimate part of the life that burns in every moment.

For fifty years we visited each other often in one place
or another for one reason or another: Madison, New
York, Paris, Lexington, Chapel Hill, Providence, Santa
Barbara, and Santa Fe. There were summer months
spent in Marshall's house as he traveled around the
world.

One winter, ten years ago, just as the new century was
beginning, Marshall and I traveled together to Nepal. We
walked the streets and byways of the slums of Pokhara,
and we lodged at the base of Machhapuchhre, the sacred mountain of the Himalayas.

There could never be an adequate farewell. I find some
solace in the note Marshall affixed to a document he
wrote three years before he died. In three typed pages
he carefully addresses what he titles "The Twilight of
My Life: An Appraisal." I keep the document as another
record of how a fortunate life has been lived. Marshall's
handwritten note captures the complexity of our fifty
years of being together. He wrote, "I regard you as a
younger brother, son, or close friend." My memory,
stronger than time.

17. My Father at Sixty-Nine

Quite often, nowadays, I open the family album I have been compiling for many years. And I turn to the photograph of my father. I photographed my father on a day when I had returned for a visit from my home in New York City. The year was 1969, and my father was in the sixty-ninth year of his life. His life would end a few months later on an autumn day as he walked from the toolshed to the tractor to make a repair.

My father died much too young. I have lamented how I might have been able to know him as I matured in my own life. I have written about his life many times, to tell others about his goodness, to maintain my contact with him.

I am now several years older than the age of my father when he passed away. I must live my life for both of us. My father's life is now in mine, just as my life will be in the lives that come after mine. The desire for life is insatiable. My father on the tractor, 1969, as I remember him. My father reminds me once again who I am.

My Father

Winter

18. Montaigne in Winter

The essay form of writing had to be invented, observes Sarah Bakewell in her book *How to Live,* and it was the sixteenth-century nobleman and wine grower Michel Eyquem de Montaigne who did so. The writing we now know as the essay is a melding of ideas and knowledge with the personal. Essential to the writing is the everyday life of the author. And the observations are compelling to us as readers because we recognize our humanity in the observations made by the essayist.

This I have attempted to do in my own writings. In giving attention to my life, to what I experience in my daily life, I have hoped to offer a mirror by which others could see their own lives. The personal life of each of us is of universal importance and consequence. We all are of this common stream of human evolution and consciousness. We all attempt to find meaning in daily existence. We learn from each other.

This journal to which I attend in some way each day helps me to be mindful in the course of my daily life. My writing is for the imagined reader at some future time as well as for myself. I sit at the dining room table this particular winter morning as the sun reflects sharply off last night's snowfall. Writing is part of my faith.

Christmas at home with love light gleaming. In the living room Al Green is singing about being home for Christmas. The night is magnified by that remembered—and imagined—place of long ago. We will be home once again, certainly in our dreams.

Blessed are we in our own ways. Yet, of personal concern this year is a hip that is causing daily pain and problems walking. Hope—with the support of family—keeps me from thinking that this is the beginning of the end. Dreams, yes, but also fears—these are the realities of the season.

The season of the solstice, fires in the night, celebration of the birth of a messiah, as well as poverty and homelessness, nations at war, lands occupied, and disease and pestilence. At Christmastime, hopefully and unreasonably, we demand a miracle in the world and in our everyday lives. Asking for what is impossible, the eternal, in the finite world. I will recite today W. H. Auden's long poem *For the Time Being: A Christmas Oratorio*. To quote the lines on the miracle that will not happen:

> We who must die demand a miracle.
> How could the Eternal do a temporal act,

The Infinite become a finite fact?
Nothing can save us that is possible:
We who must die demand a miracle.

Later in the oratorio for Christmas, Auden reminds us: "The Time Being is, in a sense, the most trying time of all." We may be waiting for the impossible to happen, but:

> In the meantime
> There are bills to be paid, machines to keep in repair,
> Irregular verbs to learn, the Time Being to redeem
> From insignificance.

In the finiteness of time, the most important task for us is to embrace fully and consciously our everyday lives.

Thy will be done here on earth. The chorus in Auden's poem directs our attention: "Love Him in the world of Flesh." We are promised rare beasts to see and unique adventures to have.

And behold, early in the morning, the message comes from my daughter Anne in a hospital in Memphis: "Baby is here. 1:30ish, 5 lbs. 8 oz. More later..." To us a baby is born. A manger, a mother and a father, and a baby born again to this wondrous, finite world.

20. The Prophet Tiresias

The prophet Tiresias appears to Odysseus in the underworld. The prophet now resides in the land of the dead, is of the dead, and appears to Odysseus as a ghost. He drinks blood from a sacrificed lamb so that all the truth can be told to Odysseus. He warns Odysseus that the journey homeward will be hard and dangerous. And at home, there will be more troubles. Once these are solved, and after a brief reunion with Penelope, there will be one more journey.

The prophet tells Odysseus that he must go forth once more, carrying his well-planed oar until he comes to a race of people who know nothing of the sea. The oar is to be planted in the earth; fine beasts are to be sacrificed to the lord of the sea; and further offerings are to be made "to the deathless gods who rule the vaulting skies, to all the gods in order." And, then, finally, the prophesying of Odysseus's death:

And at last your own death will steal upon you...
a gentle, painless death, far from the sea it comes
to take you down, borne down with the years in ripe
   old age
with all your people there is blessed peace around you.
All that I have told you will come true.

The prophet Tiresias occurs frequently as soothsayer throughout Greek mythology. The prophet figures in the classical tales of Apollo, Zeus, Athena, Oedipus, and Dionysus, among others, and continues to play a part in modern literature. Is it surprising that only now I tell you that the prophet of Thebes is a blind seer? Truth is told; the one who is without sight sees the future. And more, you should know that Tiresias was transformed into a woman for seven years.

The prophet of Thebes was blinded by the gods for revealing their secrets, for telling the truth, and was given complexity in the transformation from man to woman and back again. The prophet embodies the many oppositions—male and female, the gods and mankind, sighted and blind, present and future, and inhabiting the land of the living and the underworld of the dead. Tiresias, a prophet for all seasons. We listen when the prophet speaks.

21. Odysseus at Home

As a new year begins, January 2011, we follow happily and with considerable interest the journey of Odysseus. The journey, now that he has reached his homeland, is into the new territory of old age. Perhaps this is the most difficult journey of all. Assured by the prophet that everything is coming to pass as prophesied, we share in Penelope's wisdom: "If the gods will really grant a happier old age, there's hope that we'll escape our trials at last."

Odysseus inspires us because his story is one of quest. And in all quest stories, the trial is that the traveler will become worthy of the quest. Finally the traveler will reach the destination with dignity, compassion, and a good deal of equanimity. Not only is the end being reached, but the hero is worthy of the completion.

The focus is on the journey itself, on the living of each day. Awareness is practiced and maintained daily as the journey continues. Some alternative reality where old age and death are only temporary may cross the mind of the aging traveler, but attention always comes back to the trials of daily life. Even in pain and declining powers the hero struggles to embrace each day as it is.

22. Snowman in the Glass Ball

A winter storm this day—as the week begins—pushes across the Midwest, bringing an accumulating snow that will amount to several inches by nightfall. Temperatures are expected to fall to a record-breaking low by the end of the week. My hip is aching, my leg is failing, and I will not be able to walk more than a few steps today from one room to another. Brahms's *Requiem,* performed by the Vienna Philharmonic, fills the living room with sounds of a kind of hope even in the midst of a winter storm. I am happy!

Montaigne's often-quoted line inspires: "Life should be an aim unto itself, a purpose unto itself." It is always life that matters. Virginia Woolf was fond of quoting this thought from Montaigne. The subject of all our efforts—including these writings of mine—is this ordinary life, and the attention given to this ordinary life.

Let it flow—the life and these meandering reflections. When afternoon comes, I will watch the filmed version of Virginia Woolf's novel *Mrs. Dalloway.* A life observed in stream of consciousness, the consciousness of the writer and protagonist of the novel. Man, man alive, the snow blows across the window! I am the snowman in the glass ball. Tip me over and watch the snow fall all around me.

23. A Train in the Night

I cannot read often enough the description of traveling on the train between Chicago and Saint Paul that F. Scott Fitzgerald gives to Nick Carraway, the wonderful narrator of *The Great Gatsby*. Returning home at Christmastime, Nick is about to leave Union Station on one of the murky yellow cars of the Chicago, Milwaukee & St. Paul Railroad. He will ride through the countryside of my childhood: "When we pulled out into the winter night and the real snow, our snow, began to stretch out beside us and twinkle against the windows, and the dim lights of small Wisconsin stations moved by, a sharp wild brace came suddenly into the air. We drew in deep breaths of it as we walked back from dinner through the cold vestibules, unutterably aware of our identity with this country for one strange hour before we melted indistinguishably into it again."

This could be a train ride that I took at a time not far removed from that of Nick Carraway and the great Jay Gatsby. I am of that ride and time. I am also, with Nick and Gatsby, somewhat deficient in adapting to a worldly life east of the Midwest but aspire to a life beyond the frontier of my ancestors. Ancestors whose own dreams brought them from humble farms of England and Ireland to the New World.

24. The Golden Rule

Do you ever find yourself looking out the window late on a winter's afternoon, as the lowering sun sends a soft golden light across the crusted snow held firm throughout the day, and wonder whether all this is really true? Could all this be an illusion of a mind that is near to being overwhelmed by what can be comprehended at a single time? And what I have just seen from my window only moments ago passes as afternoon light changes and this mind finds itself with other thoughts and cares. One illusion passes into another. A life rising and falling ten thousand times each day.

I asked the doctor what the world might be like a thousand years from now—long after we have passed away. He had told me some years ago, after we had met for several sessions to talk about my concern about aging and death, that what we leave behind are the many illusions we had during our lifetime. This I would think about often since that meeting with the doctor, and the thought would be of some consolation.

The doctor still gives me counsel as we talk about the aches and pains and my personal worries about aging. As the hour goes on, with long pauses of silence as we sit across from each other, I gain insights that will guide me in the days ahead. In a few words: be compassionate toward this self of mine that is living intently and intentionally each day; what we call enlightenment is simply the alleviation of suffering; what brings me great joy and peace and comfort is the witnessing of acts of kindness, the kindness I know in others and the kindness I know in myself. The doctor gave me a prescription to follow: list daily the acts of kindness I am experiencing. For a long time—whatever else I have done—I have tried to be of help to others. The Golden Rule—a prayer for bedtime and for the waking hours as morning comes.

25. The Narrator

Do you sometimes think of your life as a story? Do you know that you are the narrator of the story of your life? When you tell others, especially when you write about your life, you are telling a story that has a certain unity, design, and rhythm. You find the patterns that have emerged in the course of your life. Maybe you have already thought about a beginning, middle, and a possible ending to the story. In all likelihood, the story of the life you have created in the living—as well as in the telling—gives meaning each day to your life and provides a guide for the days ahead. We all, as storytellers, make a story of our lives: who we are, where we came from, what we value, what we hope we can give to others, and how we can know peace of mind in our daily lives.

As we tell our stories, we necessarily return to the past. Not really return, of course, but think about the life once lived, about the people we have known, and the lives that have come before us. My philosophy tells me to live in the present moment, the only time I really have. The here and now.

And the doctor tells me that our present moments are enhanced by thoughts of the past. The past is part of the present—in mind and in concrete contemporary reality. The only nostalgia to guard against is the one that prompts the desire to still be living in the past.

Nick Carraway speaks to Jay Gatsby, who is thinking about his lost love, Daisy, as they stand on the lawn in the evening after the big party at Gatsby's mansion: "You can't repeat the past." Gatsby cries out, "Can't repeat the past? Why of course you can!" Gatsby, Fitzgerald tells us, looks around wildly, "as if the past were lurking here in the shadow of his house, just out of reach of his hand." As the novel ends, so does the life of Gatsby. Gatsby has been brought down by the dream that the past can be repeated. We in the New World still want to dream that dream. Fitzgerald ends the novel: "So we beat on, boats against the current, borne back ceaselessly into the past." The great American story, a cautionary tale.

26. Multitudes

The fragile human psyche under siege. We all are engulfed by a vast unknown. I'm reading a review of the new Russia movie *How I Ended This Summer.* The movie is about two meteorologists who are operating a weather station in the Arctic and the perils of living so far from civilization. How would we survive, removed from the protective cover of the civilized culture of books, poetry, art, and music? I realize this even more as the snow piles high against doors and windows, and the temperature and wind chill fall well below zero. Will the inner voice protect us from the elements? Fortunately, our voices are infused with a lifetime of being immersed in the comfort of cultural creations.

You can see how the writing in this commonplace book of mine is filled with references to music and to the words and images of others. It is as if I could not live without the vast and rich cultural creations that have been made for centuries, in one time or another, in one particular place or another. I am a composite—in mind and spirit and voice—of all that has come before me. And I am informed daily by what I read in the newspaper and hear on the radio. I contain multitudes, as Walt Whitman wrote in *Leaves of Grass.* I am multitudes inseparable from everything that has come before me, and I am an intimate part of everything that exists.

The afternoon sun coming through the open blinds on the south window sends shadows across the surface of my writing table. I am listening to Gustav Mahler's Ninth Symphony. How magnificent is this space I fully inhabit late on a winter's day. In his symphony, Mahler created an illusion of life everlasting. Life does seem everlasting in this present moment with music flowing gently into afternoon light. We live in the music.

27. At the Edge of a Galaxy

How many times have you gone around the sun? This is one way to think about who you are and how long you have had your feet planted on Earth. You can calculate the distance you have traveled each year of your life spinning around the sun. How many miles will you travel this day without even leaving your home? And this is not including the distance you travel as the Earth hurls outward as the universe expands.

Here we are at the edge of the Milky Way galaxy. As we have been learning daily on radio and in the papers, the space telescope Kepler is finding planets like ours supportive of life. We are reminded this morning that Earth-like planets likely exist in the other hundred billion galaxies in the universe.

In the meantime, this day, on planet Earth in the Milky Way galaxy, I savor the evening we spent with our friends Carol and Lee watching, occasionally, the Green Bay Packers play the Pittsburgh Steelers in the forty-fifth Super Bowl. A celebration of the victory of the Packers took place last night at Lambeau Field in Green Bay.

Today I am resting from yesterday's procedure at Meriter Hospital, where I underwent a fluoroscopy-guided injection and x-rays of my hip to determine the cause of pain and walking problems. Temperature will not rise above seven degrees today, but the sun is shining brightly. Chickadees, finches, a nuthatch, and a red-bellied woodpecker are at the feeder. Two squirrels are carrying away slices of old bread from the balcony, and I am seeing the early signs of mating as the squirrels dart among the branches of the locust tree.

And I have traveled far this day, moving from room to room, as the planet upon which I live spins on its axis and makes its way around the sun, and as the galaxies expand outward with the universe. Earth is moving around the sun at 62,000 miles an hour. In one year we travel 584 million miles around the sun. Today, from the time I got out of bed and made a pot of coffee to the time I will go to bed and turn off the light, I will have traveled a million miles on a yearly trip around the sun. And I, with you, have been speeding outward with the universe, to who knows where? Good reason, then, that at times we have this sense of vertigo, bewilderment, and wonder.

28. Sledding at the Farm

A joy of winter is being able to spend much of the time indoors. Inside, we know and experience the interior space—space that is physical, mental, and spiritual. Being indoors, paradoxically, prompts a movement between the inside and the outside. Within, I remember, I anticipate, and I experience a world beyond the walls of my house. My mindset is that of the traveler, traveling afar to know and appreciate what is here at home. Think of other such travelers who imagined a world from their homes: Xavier de Maistre while confined to his room; Marcel Proust alone in his apartment thinking about childhood; room-bound René Descartes creating a philosophy; Samuel Beckett looking out his window at the prison yard as he wrote; and the countless number of people anonymous and otherwise, published or unpublished, who have written notes and diaries from the quiet spaces of their inner lives. We read about our hero of travel and adventure, the great Odysseus, because the writer we know as Homer gave him life. The writer, the one who stays home at the writing desk or in bed with a pad of paper, takes us to places beyond our daily lives and confined locales.

How often at home I take flight to other times and other places. My time present, my here and now, is expanded by such travel from inside to outside. The present

Sledding at the Farm

moment of my well-being is enriched by thoughts that take me elsewhere. A winter day, and deep inside I image such a day long ago as my brother and I race down a snow-packed hill east of the barn. I imagined the scene some thirty years ago when I was living in Providence and contemplating a return to the Midwest to live on or near my family farm. I am not a drawer, but I am fascinated with the childlike drawings of artists young, old, and in between. At the time I was discovering the paintings and drawings and writings of the Canadian, of Ukrainian immigrant parents, William Kurelek. I was treasuring two of his books about growing up on the prairies of Alberta and Manitoba, *A Prairie Boy's Summer* and *A Prairie Boy's Winter*. Purchasing a book for sketching, I made several ink drawings, coloring with pencils, of events I remembered from my childhood.

In one of the drawings I am sledding down the hill east of the barn with my brother on a fine winter day. Maybe this drawing—from inside my head of that other time—was the impetus to move from the East Coast, where I had been living for many years, back to the Midwest. Not a return to my childhood, but to a present where I could discover my homeland anew, where I could know that homeland in a new way, in a way that would give new meaning to my life.

29. Inheritance

Commonplace, now, what the prophet said, that this would come to pass. I'm told by friends and acquaintances, at various turns, "It is as it is." Things are as they are. We are reminded of the song "Que Sera, Sera"—whatever will be, will be. And in the wisdom of Buddhism, be mindful and you will see all things come and all things pass away—this is the nature of the world.

A rush of multitudes. The president of Egypt has been forced to resign. Protests against autocratic regimes are taking place in several countries in the Middle East. Here in town, thousands of demonstrators are protesting a proposal by the governor to suspend the right of collective bargaining by public workers. The United States Congress is debating legislation on budget cutting. Warmer temperatures have melted some of the accumulated snow. My new grandson, Fyntan, is growing into his second month here on Earth in Memphis, Tennessee. Valentine's Day has come and gone. My sore hip keeps me at home, away from demonstrating at the capitol. And, once again, I'm listening to John Cale sing his song "I Keep a Close Watch" and keeping a close watch on this heart of mine.

I have made contact with descendants, heretofore unknown, of our farm family. We had lost the trail of the descendants of Tom and Florence Quinney in South Dakota. And only recently have I found the descendants of my mother's great-grandparents James and Joyce Wishart, many now living in southern Minnesota. That I am of Scottish descent, from the Wisharts, is a fairly recent discovery about my origins. Behind my investigations into family history there is the attempt to place myself in the larger world, a world that included the emigration of my family from the Old World.

Oh, the seriousness of these thoughts. Stacked on the table are several diaries and notebooks handwritten by my ancestors, writings that have survived many moves and dispersals: the notes kept by my great-grandfather Holloway as he sailed from England in the mid-nineteen century; the sparse diary kept by my great-aunt Kate late in her life; entries in a notebook about the first months of my father's life made by his mother; a farm ledger kept by my grandfather Holloway; and a notebook of addresses and birth dates from the desk of my mother.

And then there is the small, red, cloth-covered album with entries made in the month of February 1891. Here are the signatures and verses written by friends and relatives of my grandmother Hattie, my father's mother before her marriage to John Quinney. She would have been twenty-one years old at the time of the album. Bridget Quinney, who emigrated from Ireland during the famine, makes an entry in Hattie's little book:

When hearts whose truth was proven
Like thine, are laid in earth.
There should a wreath be woven
To tell the world their worth.

We descendants of those who ventured to a new land
inherit a very serious nature.

30. Tom and Florence in South Dakota

In the same album of 1891, Tom Quinney, my father's uncle, signs his name in a fine hand, after inscribing, "All that glitters is not gold." Tom would have been on a return visit to the home place in Wisconsin from his new home in South Dakota. Exactly eleven years earlier, also in the month of February, he would have been in the middle of a blizzard, making his way through the snow to claim land for a homestead.

For the first time in our family history, only this morning, I have made contact with Tom's great-granddaughter. After reaching her in Minnesota on the telephone and introducing ourselves to each other, we talked about Tom's arduous journey to South Dakota in the winter of 1880. We both had read the account of Tom's son, Elwin, that was published in an 1899 book on the prominent old settlers of South Dakota.

Starting from Whitewater, a few miles north and west of the Old Place, on February 15, Tom and his friend C. H. Nott traveled by rail to Algona, Iowa. Caught in a snowstorm, the train and passengers were blockaded for four days. After shoveling snow, they pushed on to Emmetsburg. Tom developed back trouble and was forced to lie quietly in a hotel for two weeks. Pressing on by train, the travelers were again blocked by snow, on their run to Mitchell, South Dakota. Tom and Nott were now discouraged of reaching their destination by rail and, finding their funds running low, decided to walk. Pushing out across the snow-covered prairie, with the white unbroken expanse reflecting painfully the sunlight, they were snow blind by the time they reached Marion Junction. Somehow, the men continued on the next morning, groping blindly in strange country and without even so much as a trail to follow.

As they struggled on, sustained by hardened snow crust, but suddenly sinking where the tall grass had weakened the crust, Tom and his companion stumbled up the hills and plunged through the ravines, until finally they heard, from a distance, a man calling his cattle. By calls and answers, they succeeded in reaching him and passed the night in his shanty. The next morning, not yet recovered from their snow blindness, they hired the man to lead them to the Barker brothers, old friends of theirs in Wisconsin who lived but a few miles away.

As soon as Tom and his friend recovered from the effects of their walk in the snow, they went to Mitchell and filed their homestead claims. After purchasing three dollars' worth of roof boards for their sod shanty, a sack of flour, and a jug of molasses, they took inventory of their cash and found they had just fourteen cents.

A year after claiming the land for a homestead, Tom married Florence Loomer, a childhood friend. They raised a family, and in time, we are told in the account of pioneers, obtained a comfortable life.

Tom died in the winter of 1924. Florence occasionally returned to Wisconsin to visit our family. Each time that she came to visit us at the farm she brought a book for my brother and me. Often I reach to the shelf of the bookcase and open one of the books signed "From Aunt Florence."

31. The Things I Know

John Quinney, Tom's brother and my grandfather, also inscribed a verse to Hattie in her album of 1891. In three years, John and Hattie would be married. John's inscription gives Hattie his reference of character. He wrote:

I Dont go much on religion
I never aint had no Show
But Ive got a middlin tight grip Sir
On the handful of things I Know.

Humble in character, but with a resolve that could be depended upon in matters essential.

Hattie passed away, from consumption, after ten years of marriage and the birth of three children. John continued to farm and never married again. My father told me that he always told him that he would never again find a woman as good as Hattie.

32. The Unborn

In these ancestral and family stories that I tell, accounts that I find meaningful to my life, I need to keep perspective. I need to be well aware of the mind that is creating these stories and not lose my true self in the drama of the storytelling. Stories give temporal meaning to our lives, but we are always more than the stories we tell. We all have a true nature—a truth—that is absolute and beyond the relativity of our conscious lives.

This ultimate reality that encompasses our relative existence is what Zen masters for centuries have called the *unborn*. Our original and everlasting self, our *unborn* nature. This unborn that is known to us through the writings of Zen master Bankei of the seventeenth century. Where were you before you were born? This question gives some comfort as the body shows daily signs of aging.

Patience—and happiness—as I sit quietly at the table after the night of falling snow. Meditate—be still—in the unborn realm of this infinite and pervasive original mind. My life among the multitude of lives in a universe that is itself finite. *Samadhi* is the Sanskrit word for this composure of mind and body. Moments where you sense the greater reality. Where wisdom and compassion can be found, can be known and practiced in daily life.

Be careful of dwelling entirely in the constructed stories of our lives and those of our ancestors. At the same time that these stories are being imagined and told, be mindful that they can put us in a dream world apart from who we really are. The stories can separate us from the wholeness of our original nature. And be careful of the stories of loss and sorrow that will cause suffering of the mind. A lament for what no longer exists, a sorrow over the passing of others and other times, will certainly bring suffering.

But we are human, human beings in a long line of the evolution of this life form. And the experience of suffering is part of our humanity. Not to end all suffering, a human impossibility, but to be aware of it. Be mindful that the past, present, and future are of the same moment.

We move many times daily between a dream world, our constructed reality, and a fleeting glimpse of ultimate reality, the unbornness of our existence. This is one of the great wonders of being human. We are here and elsewhere simultaneously, and sometimes we are consciously aware of this, however fleetingly. Maintaining our balance is another creative adjustment to being human.

Some reminders help us—flash cards, quotations, pictures, and prayers. For me, often, my instruction is from the allegory of the oxherd. I imagine, seeing from

the back of my temporal mind, the herding of the ox—
the cow—in the pasture at the farm. Midway across the
field, I release my hold on the cow I am herding, and
we begin to walk together in harmony. The beast, my
mind and the cow, has been tamed. No longer the di-
vision, the struggle, between herder and cow. We have
become one and the same, and are on the way home.
I will go on telling stories—and living this human and
temporal life—but sometimes with the awareness and
perspective of the unborn.

33. Scrapbook

We in Wisconsin have been in the national news, and the international news, for the last week and a half. The governor insists on restricting the rights of workers to negotiate, and it is becoming clear that this is part of the conservative agenda throughout the country. How this will play out is the unknown of the day. I must watch and listen from home because of my inability to walk up the steps of the capitol building. I await appointments with doctors.

Stored in the music cabinet that stood for fifty years on the front porch of the farmhouse are some of the scrapbooks from my mother's childhood. Now I am the keeper of the music cabinet and the scrapbooks. Each time I page through them, as I am doing today, I am struck by the fact that I am seeing some of the things that my mother valued. During her young years she placed into scrapbooks the images, from greeting cards and magazines, that she found beautiful and meaningful to her life. Throughout her life—into her nineties—she had a scrapbook nearby and ready for another picture to be savored and saved. I see now what my mother once saw with her eyes, and cared for. I keep nearby her childhood scrapbook, the book of pictures that she gave to me when I was born.

34. Telling the Story

I am your narrator—the teller of the story and the spin-ner of tales within the story. I am in the time-honored tradition of the first-person narrator. My narration is also of the subjective mode. Adding to all of this, my telling is a stream of consciousness. And necessarily dictated by the form, I am your "unreliable" narrator. With great seriousness, I am trying to tell you what is happening.

No pretension of being an omniscient observer. I am the first-person narrator with a lifetime of experience that determines what I am seeing now and what I am remembering of the past. As soon as I put my pen to paper, I am in the realm of fiction. In this sense, there is no such thing as nonfiction and no observation that can be objective. The narrator is the main character in the story.

Think of yourself, as you tell the story, as being like one of the pilgrims in Chaucer's *Canterbury Tales*. Or Huck in Mark Twain's *Adventures of Huckleberry Finn*. Or the longtime acquaintance of the old soldier in Ford Madox Ford's *Good Soldier*. Or one of the family mem-bers carrying the mother's body on the wagon in William Faulkner's *As I Lay Dying*. Or one of the townspeople in Fellini's film *Amarcord* or one of the observers in Kurosawa's *Rashomon*, which fifty years ago set me on my course of searching for the multiple realities in the world of everyday life. I can see no other way of being in the world and surviving to tell about it.

Writing in a journal, keeping a diary or daybook, is a presentation of the interior life of the writer. An interior monologue, a stream of consciousness, is being recorded. The emotional, intellectual, and spiritual life of the writer is being displayed to the prospective reader of the journal. Trust that your storyteller is trying to the best of his or her ability to inform you.

Narrators may well be on a path of increasing awareness of themselves and the world around them as they tell their stories. The narrator is becoming mindful, giving attention to the mind that is narrating the story. The mind is being watched as the writing, the telling, is taking place. Writing has become a form of meditation. The examined mind, in the course of storytelling, is part of the process of being compassionate. This is the Buddhist meditation, and the practice, of the storyteller.

35. A Home on the Range

In my box of materials from the early years is the Sears Home Study Course for Spanish Guitar. In seventh or eighth grade, I had hopes of learning how to play the guitar. I had visions of cowboys singing in the saddle as they herded cows on the range. Sixty complete lessons are contained in the bright yellow and blue spiral-bound book.

A few months ago I spoke about the old days to a Monday morning gathering of graduates of Delavan High School. I mentioned my early guitar lessons with a teacher with an Old World accent. Once a week I would have a lesson in his living room in the Temperance House apartments on West Walworth Avenue. I learned to play and sing "A Home on the Range," lesson no. 36, and imagined myself a cowboy herding cattle on the range.

> Oh, give me a home where the buffalo roam,
> Where the deer and the antelope play,
> Where seldom is heard a discouraging word
> And the skies are not cloudy all day.

After trying for years to recall my guitar teacher's name, I appealed to Gordon Yadon, the local historian in Delavan. He came up with the name Bruno Kupher,

A Home on the Range

a music teacher who had come to Delavan in the mid-1930s, probably with support from a federal program for the arts during the Depression. He continued to offer music lessons at various locations in town. An entry for the Kupher family, Gordon told me, ceased to exist in the Delavan directory early in the 1950s.

Failing to ride on my horse and play the guitar at the same time, I turned to the ukulele, an instrument of four strings rather than six. I still have the book, *New Ukulele Method* by May Singhi Breen, for beginners and advanced students. The last song to be learned in the book is "When the Moon Comes over the Mountain."

In his introduction to the ukulele instruction book, musician and bandleader Paul Whiteman expressed his wish to have the ukulele adopted everywhere and commended May Singhi Breen ("the Ukulele Lady") for her "sincere efforts to have the ukulele recognized as a standard musical instrument." The ukulele still fills a niche in contemporary music. One of the most watched Internet sites is a rendition of George Harrison's song "While My Guitar Gently Weeps" being played in Central Park by a master of the instrument. In the meantime, knowing that not everything material can be saved, I threw my aging ukulele into the dumpster as the farmhouse attic was being emptied. But the desire to play, at home on the range, remains.

Nina Simone is singing "I'm not over you for a while." Days go by ... people say to me you need company ... when you have some time ... when you need a friend ... not over you for a while. What is a day without a ballad, especially late in the afternoon as winter's sun moves higher in the sky with each passing day? Two house finches, male and female, perch on the branch just outside my window. Yesterday Solveig told me that she had heard birds singing.

In the darkened theater earlier this week, I was able to scribble some of the lyrics from the opera based on President Nixon's trip to China in 1972. It was *Nixon in China,* by John Adams, shown at the movie theater in a simulcast production from the Metropolitan Opera in New York. The soprano portraying Pat Nixon sings at the gate of Longevity and Goodwill, "Let routine dull the edge of mortality." She also observes, "This is prophetic!" before going on to the Ming Tombs. At the end of the opera, Chou En-lai wonders about the goodness of what has been done.

Newspapers report the passing of the woman who, now famously, held onto Bob Dylan's arm as they walked on a slushy Jones Street in Greenwich Village in the winter of 1963. We know the photograph from the cover of the record album. Dylan would soon write the song "Don't Think Twice, It's Alright," a lament while the woman was away in Italy visiting family. Suze Rotolo wrote her own book, *A Freewheelin' Time*, about her years with Dylan. I'll read the book soon, and it will be another chance for me to think about my life when I lived in New York near the street where Dylan and Rotolo walked arm in arm on a winter's day.

37. A Painting in Delavan

In the routine and on the edge again. The day is to be filled with medical appointments — going to the clinics of interventional spine specialist, optometrist, and gastroenterologist. And then a few notes for the day in my journal on this bright March day.

Delavan historian Gordon Yadon has given me more information about the framed painting that I took to the Monday morning gathering several months ago. Gordon has written several articles over the years in the local newspaper on the artist Adolph Shulz. Born in Delavan in 1869, Shulz hiked the woods and fields of Wisconsin making sketches. He went on to study art in Chicago, New York, Paris, and Munich. He married another young artist, Ada Walter, and they had a son. Beginning in 1892, students from the Art Institute of Chicago came to Delavan in the summertime to paint with the Shulzes. In 1917, Adolph and Ada moved to the emerging art colony in Indiana's Brown County. In 1926, Adolph left the marriage for another artist, Alberta Rehm.

The landscape and portrait paintings, impressionistic in style, of the three artists are being newly found, restored, and purchased by collectors and museums. Abrams Public Library in Delavan holds some of the paintings. Occasionally, there is news that another painting by one of the Shulzes has been found.

The twenty or so summers of painting in Delavan, with students coming to learn and practice their art, is part of the local lore. We imagine their time together, summering and painting and doing things that caught the imagination.

I asked Gordon about the framed painting that I had purchased in the early 1980s at a yard sale in Delavan. I wondered if the painting could be the work of one of the summer students. It looks like something a student would paint while studying the work of a Dutch master. Gordon tells me that such paintings often turn up at yard sales in Delavan. He has graciously invited me to borrow and copy from his extensive files on the Shulzes and their years of living and painting in Delavan. A record of the artistic life, once upon a time, in my hometown.

38. Old Age

I review the instructions for the upper GI endoscopy scheduled for later this week. "Plan ahead. You will be given sedatives, which can greatly affect your judgment. On the day of your test, you will not be able to drive or return to work."

In the current issue of the *New Yorker*, Jill Lepore writes about the meeting of the psychologists G. Stanley Hall, Carl Jung, and Sigmund Freud in 1909 at Hall's home in Worcester, Massachusetts. Hall, with keen sensitivity to his own biography, studied the early years, adolescence, and old age. One period of life was the flip side of the other. Lepore writes: "Either you're growing up or you're growing down. For him, there was very little in between. Old age takes everyone by surprise, and no one really ever comes to terms with it. Hall thought that this was because old age is the only stage of life we never grow out of, and can never look back on, not on this earth, anyway."

As we are getting older, we don't know where we are going. Hall suggested that at such time we should think about where we came from. Do I not, in this journal, often look back to where I came from? If I am not to know where I am going, I can find some satisfaction in knowing about, and possibly understanding better, the life I have lived up to this time. At what point am I, are any of us, prepared to say to others and to ourselves that we are now old? Am I ready to declare that I am an old man? Psychologically, and spiritually, I am still in resistance. Physically, the reality is fast approaching or already here.

39. Zen Gleanings

On the cusp of seasons, most exciting. Winter fast fading, winter waning—winter waned. Spring is about to arrive. A sure sign: the turkey vultures have returned. They soar and glide and circle high in the sky, cruising for carrion and refuse, tilting gently from side to side. I count thirteen circling over the woods east of the house. They have scented winter's kill, and will devour and cleanse the ruins of winter. I welcome once again the return of the vultures.

My gleaning throughout the winter has been reading, at bedtime, from the anthology of contemporary Buddhist wisdom—*The Buddha Is Still Teaching,* edited by Jack Kornfield. A listing at winter's end of a few spiritual passages I have noted, inspirations before the coming of dreams.

Our personal experiences of pain and joy, grief and despair, may be unique to each of us in the forms they take, yet our capacity to feel grief, fear, loneliness, and rage, as well as delight, intimacy, joy, and ease, are our common bonds as human beings.— *Christina Feldman*

Even the most difficult problems, such as serious illness and the decay of the body as it ages, can be viewed positively. We tend to see "self" as permanent, but in fact self, with all its cravings and clingings, is not solid. When pain comes, all our illusions crumble and are swept away like a sand castle being washed out to sea with the first big wave. Family, house, career, all the cherishable things of life, will disappear some day. —*Tulku Thondup*

If everything is noted, all your emotional difficulties will disappear. When you feel happy, don't get involved with the happiness. And when you feel sad, don't get involved with it. Whatever comes, don't worry. Just be aware of it. —*Dipa Ma*

The basic teaching of Buddhism is the teaching of transiency, or change. That everything changes is the basic truth for each existence. No one can deny this truth, and all the teaching of Buddhism is condensed within it. —*Shunryu Suzuki*

Did we learn to live through the changes of life with grace, wisdom, and compassion? Have we learned to shift from the clinging mind to the joy of freedom? —*Jack Kornfield*

Each time my feet touched the earth, I knew my mother was there with me. I knew this body was not mine alone but a living continuation of my mother and my father and my grandparents and great-grandparents. Of all my ancestors. These feet that I saw as "my" feet were actually "our" feet. — *Thich Nhat Hanh*

Buddha Dharma does not teach that everything is suffering. What Buddhism does say is that life, by its nature, is difficult, flawed, and imperfect. — *Lama Surya Das*

That I might be aware and open to the experiences of daily life is a bedtime prayer. From a night of dream and illusion, I will awaken to a new day. And be aware of the wonders that the day will hold.

Spring

40. Vernal Equinox

Spring of 2011 came late in the afternoon. In the darkening sky, early evening, lightning flashed and thunder cracked, and a heavy rain began to fall and water rushed down the street and soaked the lawn just cleared of winter's blanket of snow. Such rain and water have not been seen since the beginning of winter. Late into the night, I watched Visconti's film *Death in Venice,* based on Thomas Mann's novel. A musical score drawn from Mahler's Third and Fifth symphonies haunted the film from beginning to end.

And this morning brings the first full day of spring. The sun, although obscured by cloud and fog, is directly overhead at the equator. At the vernal equinox, when day and night are of approximately equal length, the sun crosses the celestial equator going northward, rising exactly due east and setting exactly due west. There is order, established again this day, in the universe.

The weather report today: Storms moving in from the Rockies could become severe in the Plains and Upper Midwest from Nebraska to Wisconsin, by evening. Warming temperatures will spread across the East as the early spring storm tracks over the Appalachians toward the coast. Thunderstorms are predicted along the Mason-Dixon line. The local forecast for the rest of the week promises a mix of rain and snow.

If we can see the full moon tonight, with an occasional clearing between the clouds, the moon will be the closest to Earth it has been in eighteen years.

The full moon of 2011 is only 221,567 miles from Earth, compared to the average distance of 238,000 miles. Astrologers have linked supermoons to natural disasters. But scientists have been assuring us that this is not the case with this month's earthquake off the coast of Japan, accompanied by a twenty-foot tsunami and destruction to nuclear power plants. A disaster for us here on Earth—with or without a supermoon.

41. Call of the Sirens

As dawn with her rose-red fingers shone again, the lustrous goddess Circe warmly hailed Odysseus and his shipmates: "Ah my daring, reckless friends! You who have ventured down to the House of Death alive." She offers food and wine and rest for the livelong day. Taking Odysseus aside, she warns him of the island of the Sirens that his ship must pass on the return to Ithaca. The Sirens—the singing creatures of Greek mythology that beckon sailors to their deaths—are to be avoided.

Odysseus's ship approaches the island, and as the ship is about to pass, the Sirens burst into their high, thrilling song: "Come closer, famous Odysseus—Achaea's pride and glory—moor your ship on our coast so you can hear our song! Never has any sailor passed our shores in his black craft until he has heard the honeyed voices pouring from our lips, and once he hears to his heart's content sails on, a wiser man."

But Odysseus heeds Circe's warning that the singing is a ruse to lure sailors to their deaths. Odysseus tells his men to put wax in their ears so they will not hear the Sirens. He orders his men to bind him to the ship's mast so that he will not go to the Sirens when he hears their song. When the island has been passed and the singing of the Sirens is out of range, Odysseus is freed from the mast. Homer gives us Odysseus's own words, for us to read centuries later: "But once we'd left the Sirens fading in our wake, once we could hear their song no more, their urgent call—my steadfast crew was quick to remove the wax I'd used to seal their ears and loosed the bonds that lashed me." Courage, presence of mind, tactics, and the help of the goddess once again saved Odysseus and his crew.

With some imagination, I am being called by the alluring voices of the Sirens. A year ago Laurie Lewis signed for me a copy of her new CD, *Blossoms,* during the intermission of her performance at the High Noon Saloon. Solveig purchased the CD for me, and we chatted with Laurie and her husband, Tom Roxum, who accompanied her on guitar and mandolin all evening. Playing—right now—is the final song on the CD, "Sirens." Laurie sings, "Somewhere out there I hear the Sirens sing, come on, let go, give in." In another verse she makes her choice: "I stop my ears, for I have made my choice. But oh, the song is so tender." Still, at the end of the song, the Sirens continue to beckon: "Come join our song within the deep green blue." And this is just one of Laurie's songs that beckons me from afar, another island of singing voices that I must pass as I sail on.

A song that was popular the year I graduated from high school in Delavan was "You Belong to Me." The singer reminds the one he loves that whatever he is seeing, that person is part of the experience. "See the pyramids along the Nile, watch the sunrise from a tropic isle." Several versions reached the charts in the summer of 1952, a summer I remember fondly. The recordings I remember well were by Patti Page, Jo Stafford, and Dean Martin. Songs such as this one continue to draw me to places beyond everyday life. But songs—of heart and mind—that give gravitas to the days as they go by.

42. Spring Comes to the Marsh

When spring comes each year, my thoughts turn to the marsh on the farm. Wherever I have lived, the marsh has been my image of spring.

Spring was, as it still is at the marsh, the warmth of new life spreading over the land as the sun reached higher each day into the sky. Red-winged blackbirds, the first of the birds to return, perched on the cattails. The hills sloping to the marsh began to turn green with fresh and tender grass. In the woods the shooting stars raised their heads toward the sun. The mandrake plant spread its leaves over the early-forming fruit. On the hill north of the marsh the soft leaves of the mullein pushed through the earth. Over the far horizon to the south, great blue herons returned to build their nests in the tamarack trees.

As the spring night unfolded, frogs at the edge of the pond began to peep and croak. The shrill sounds of nighthawks fell sharply through the sky. A pair of red-tailed hawks nested in one of the tall oak trees. Muskrats, after resting during the long winter, emerged from their thatched houses at the edge of the marsh. Shaking the water from their furry bodies, they sunned themselves for a while, then slipped back into the water and swam away into the reeds and cattails.

The Marsh

I grew to love the marsh and all its creatures and living things. In the years of travel that would follow, what I had learned here would serve me well. I was changing then, as I am changing now, and I am still awed by the mystery of the marsh. This is the renewal, and the growth, that I know when spring comes each year after the long winter. My artist friend Lissa McLaughlin has made for me a collage of spring coming to the marsh when I was young.

43. The Daily News

The world outside, a benchmark—as my journal takes a life of its own. The international headlines will date us, as they declare the current state of our existential condition. Elizabeth Taylor, lustrous pinnacle of Hollywood glamour, dies at age seventy-nine. Allies are split over the final goal of the mission in Libya. With thousands in the streets, Syrian forces kill protesters. Japanese officials are encouraging evacuation of a wider area around the damaged nuclear power plant. Rebels in Libya make new gains amid airstrikes. Opposition forces in Ivory Coast make major gains. Drug wars push deeper in Central America. Rights group accuses Ugandan police of torture and killings. Insurgents kidnap dozens in northeast Afghanistan. Chinese democracy activist is given a ten-year sentence. The Japanese crisis revives the U.S. fight on nuclear waste. And locally, in this state of Wisconsin, there is a movement to recall the governor.

In this household, there is the right hip that needs surgery. Moving from doctor to doctor, from one diagnostic procedure to another, the consensus is that I must have surgery. While I am at the mercy of scheduling, my travels are confined to limping from one room to another. But, often, I feel that this is all of the travel I need, and I know that I am thankful for this travel.

Until the day of surgery, my sketches of daily life will be of other topics and events.

Always is the blessing of knowing that my life is a continuation of the lives of my mother and father and of all the ancestors before me. They are missed—the parents and grandparents and great-grandparents—but I am cognizant of the fact that they continue to live in my life and in the lives of my children and grandchildren. Each step that I take, from room to room, is a step that I am taking with multitudes of lives, related to me in various ways and degrees. This includes the whole of humanity, and the whole of all creatures, and likely the trees in the forests and the stones in the fields.

And in the midst of all this is the mystery of time passing. Each day passes into another. We give thanks for the ability—even with its implicit sorrow—to pay attention to the passing of our days, moment by moment being aware of our human condition.

44. Dunham School

Each spring, as the snow melts and water begins to flow, I recall the daily adventure of going to Dunham School in the morning and returning home in the afternoon. Ralph, my brother, and I, when not riding our bicycles, would walk, making our way across the field and through the woods to the school a mile away, or by way of the gravel road, a distance of a mile and a half. After the long winter, and with the warming of the days, water flowed beneath the cracking ice and hardened snow, down hillsides, and along the edges of the road. One day, I remember well, I sang all the way to school, "Oh what a beautiful morning."

Two recesses a day, plus the noon hour, gave us time for play. Boys and girls together, on a baseball field well worn from seventy-five years of play, would bat the ball and run the bases until the school bell called us back to our desks. Often we would ride the aging merry-go-round, swinging around and around and rocking back and forth until it nearly fell off its center pole. Other days we would play Andy-over-the-Schoolhouse, one team throwing the ball high over the roof and tagging each other to increase our team size in the course of the game. One warm spring day, with the smell of peanut butter and jam sandwiches still hanging in the noon-time air, we built a grass house over a structure of fallen branches. Some older students later boasted about doing unusual things in the darkness of the grass house.

And each spring, the country school superintendent, Ella Jacobson, visited our school and noted our progress. Studying and learning at Dunham School set the course for the rest of my life. Miss Jacobson wrote these encouraging words on my report card: "Every time I visit this school I find you doing good work. Always do your very best in everything you do. This will bring you success, and you will be happy in your work."

In the spring of 1947, at the end of my seventh grade, only five students remained at Dunham School. The school had to be closed until there were more students. I completed the eighth grade at Island School in Richmond Township. Ralph and I walked west through fields and woods to reach the school. That year, for the first time in my life, I felt the stressful reality of change. The transfer to Island School marked the very beginning of my move away from home.

The anticipation, and then the first sightings of green shoots coming from the wintering bulbs in the now warming ground. No wonder Easter is the designated springtime event. A resurrection for what seemed to be a death. All around, the stirrings of new life, of life restored. What appeared to be gone is here again.

And I reach again out of need to the high shelf for my daughter Laura's book *William Blake on Self and Soul*. It contains startling photographs of the life mask of Blake, eyes closed to protect the subject from the drying plaster. Inwardness personified. I must explore once more this self of mine, this self that is connected to everything beyond itself.

Blake's essential concern is the loneliness of the self, of the soul, because of the subjectivity of the individual. In all of his prophetic writings and drawings, he sought to repair the deep ontological wound. The emotion of "homesickness," the feeling of wandering adrift, is a separation from the transcendent. Such is our existential alienation in the world of everyday life.

Blake gives little thought to an afterlife. The soul is already divine, here and now. This is a new way of living our lives, where the transcendent is immanent. The achievement of the mature soul is to realize that we live in the Eternal Now. We do not wait for a reunion with the divine, with infinitude; the union already exists in our lives every day. Our recognition of the transcendent soul gives us access not to the promise of immortality but to the Eternal Now.

At the end of his long prophetic poem *Jerusalem,* Blake begins not with self-transformation, but with love. The inner self turns toward the other. This becomes the true divinity, the capacity of self-sacrifice. These words in the poem capture the significance of our union with others, the "sacrifice" that is made: "Every kindness to another is a little Death." This is a redefinition of the biblical *agape.* Our true humanity comes in self-sacrifice, when love comes first.

We hope to realize this love and the soul's transformation to the Eternal. Laura ends her book by reflecting on Blake's final, skeptical thought, with this startling line: "Perhaps the self can neither perfectly right itself nor set itself free from the essential claustrophobia of subjectivity." Maybe this is what it means to be human.

46. Wingra Walk

I can mark to the day the event that signaled a change in my life. Four years ago, on this day in April, I walked into the oak savanna a few blocks from my house. I walked through the stands of white and bur oaks and the thickets of dogwood and aspen and willow on my way to photograph along the marshy shore of the shallow lake called Wingra. Finding the location I wanted to capture on film, I set up the tripod, attached the medium format camera, framed the view to my liking, and released the shutter from the cable in my hand. The sense, once again, known so many times before, of an order in the world revealed. I knew that eventually I would have a print of something that was true, a visual record as proof of a reality and my place in it.

Then, stepping back from the camera, I tripped on a protruding root, lost my balance, and fell to the ground. Trying to get up from the fall, I wondered if the task could be accomplished. I realized, then, that photographing alone in the woods, unaccompanied, was a risk I could no longer take. I would now ask for the company of others when photographing in the woods away from home.

I have the print of the photograph made that day when I awakened to my current status in the world. You see the aging and dying trees beside the lake. A wooden

Wingra Walk

path of planks has been laid down to guide walkers over the marshy ground. A path has been provided for those who might not otherwise make their way to the other side of the woods. The photographer found satisfaction on a walk in the woods one day in spring.

47. Journey to a Far Place

The theme of journey runs through most memoirs. The life of the author is a journey marked by a progression of events and personal awakenings over the course of time. Physical distance in travel is a metaphor for the development of a life. The metaphor of journey places the life in perspective and gives it coherence. Often the author of the memoir consciously lives his or her life as a journey.

Years ago I told of my early life as "a journey to a far place." The "far place," ironically, was the home where I started, a very near place. I had traveled to a place, in my mind, where I knew something about where I came from and where I was going.

I have recently found the poem "Ithaka," by the Greek poet C. P. Cavafy. He was born in Alexandria, Egypt, where his Greek parents had settled. After living in England and working in the family business, he returned to Alexandria and worked for thirty years as a clerk and assistant director in the Ministry of Public Works. In one of Cavafy's most acclaimed poems, he gives us the essence of Homer's *Odyssey*. Our hero, Odysseus, is given instruction by the poet:

Keep Ithaka always in your mind.
Arriving there is what you're destined for.

But don't hurry the journey at all.
Better if it lasts for years,
so you're old by the time you reach the island,
wealthy with all you've gained on the way,
not expecting Ithaka to make you rich.

Yes, the journey itself is the objective, the journey taking precedence over the destination. This is a blessing: a journey lasting for a long time. A journey where your home, the place from where you began, has served you well. Served you well because it was origin and destination all in one.

48. A Stranger Walks into Town

A day of music. We drive north on a sunny Sunday afternoon to the rural village of Roxbury. The Madison Mellophonium Jazz Orchestra will be playing in the ballroom area of the Dorf Haus. The orchestra—a big band of twenty-five musicians gathered for the occasion—will be playing the original arrangements from the Stan Kenton band. Former Kenton musician from the 1960s Joel Kaye, up from Florida, will be leading the band.

The elaborate arrangements of orchestral proportion filled the room of dancers aged fifty through eighty-five, swinging, swaying, and swooping across the floor. "Moonlight Becomes You," "Misty," "Stardust," "Sophisticated Lady," "Laura," "Begin the Beguine," "Bewitched," "Spring Is Here," and more, all afternoon. Solveig and I sat at our table, with families of the band members, remembering other times when we had danced (and when I had once played in a little dance band), and enjoyed the music on a Sunday afternoon.

This morning, from the community radio station, is a live performance by street musician David Sewell. In a folk and country mode he plays and sings a Jimmie Rodgers song, "Blue Yodel No. 7."

> I was a stranger passing thru your town
> When I asked you a favor, good gal, you turned me down.

Followed by a yodel. The protagonist in the song tells us that we may see him walking down the railroad track. And that he may not be coming back.

I glance to the wall and study again the print I bought years ago in the seventeenth-century tower that W. B. Yeats restored and lived in, and wrote many of his poems in, outside the Irish town of Gort. The print is from a lithograph by his brother, Jack Yeats, and is hand colored by members of the Yeats family. It is titled "The Village." A stranger walks into town. Often I have imagined myself, with pleasure, as a stranger coming into town, even when entering my own hometown. That the sketch is in the Ireland of my ancestors gives further meaning to the image that hangs on the wall.

49. John Muir

Each time I explore the life of John Muir I find myself in a different place. A new documentary about his
life has been presented on PBS's *American Masters* series, titled "John Muir in the New World." I watched
the portrayal earlier this week, and for the rest of the
week I have been pulling from the shelves John Muir
books, and thinking about his life and his mission.
That he grew up on a farm in Wisconsin, after emigrating from Scotland with his parents in 1849, during
the same migration of my ancestors, adds to my iden-
tification with him.

Muir remained deeply religious throughout his life,
moving from the Christian theology of supernatural deity to a religion grounded in nature. In the tradition of
the transcendentalists, especially Henry David Thoreau,
Muir respected and revered nature and found human
salvation and redemption in oneness with nature and
in the protection of the natural world.

As a young man, Muir walked a thousand miles on a
journey that took him to the Gulf of Mexico. He con-
tracted malaria at the end of the walk, then booked
passage to New York and sailed to California in 1868,
where his immense life was lived until his death in 1914.
His legacy is assessed at the end of the recent biography by Donald Worster: "Muir was a man who tried

to find the essential goodness of the world, an optimist about people and nature, an eloquent prophet of a new world that looked to nature for its standard and inspiration. Looking back at the trail he blazed, we must wonder how far we have yet to go."

Muir made a sketch of sleeping on a grave in Bonaventure Cemetery near Savannah. The following morning he wrote in his journal about the fear of death. He commented on the morbid "death orthodoxy" of civilized Christian religion, observing the rituals and ceremonies that are "haunted by imaginary glooms and ghosts of every degree." What the night in the cemetery, sleeping on the grave, revealed to him, in contrast, was that death is an integral part of nature, as part of the renewing cycle of nature. He wrote this about his new understanding of death: "Let children walk with Nature, let them see the beautiful blendings and communions of death and life, their joyous inseparable unity, as taught in woods and meadows, plains and mountains and streams of our blessed star, and they will learn that death is stingless indeed, and as beautiful as life, and that the grave has no victory, for it never fights." And he added a line now famous and much quoted: "All is divine harmony."

50. As It Is in Heaven

Easter weekend begins with the Swedish movie *As It Is in Heaven*. Its relevant passage is "There is no death." The speaker voices the desire to feel, to feel with full awareness, that there is life, that life is being lived. Of solace is the idea that death is a limited notion of our existence, perhaps another of our illusions.

We of family on Easter afternoon drive to the nearby savanna of tall oaks and winding paths leading to the shore of the marshy waters. I remain at the edge of the savanna with my camera in hand and look into the trees. With bliss and abandon, and a sense of great blessing, I photograph the horizon of trees spreading against the panoramic sky of constantly changing springtime clouds.

In the evening, I read some of the haiku poems in *A Net of Fireflies,* translated by Harold Stewart and published in 1960. The two-line poems in the first section are about spring. A rebirth poem by Mokuin:

> Ah, for the heart whose winter knew no doubt,
> The white plum-blossoms, first to venture out!

I have watched treetops merge into the springtime sky.

51. Bedrock

You will see the exposed bedrock just a few blocks from my house. Follow the trail east along the former railroad bed and you will come upon the park created in the 1930s. Designed by the landscape architect Jens Jensen as an area for children, the park retains the natural features of the original landscape. A ravine cuts through the landscape, exposing the bedrock upon which the city rests. Tall black locust trees grow on the hills and slopes. At the far end of the park, high on a conical hill, is the council ring Jensen designed where children can sit on stones that circle the fire pit. Jensen repeated the council ring several times in other designs as a place where people could gather in communion. He combined elements of his native Danish folk tradition with the council fires of Native Americans and the prairie fires of the pioneers. The common good is grounded in nature.

On a spring morning a couple of years ago, I walked to the children's park, camera and tripod in hand. I photographed from the bedrock up to the council ring on the hill. There were the remnants of stick houses where children had explored and played. A sense of a return to nature—of being immersed in the natural world— impresses the mind and heart of anyone who passes by and lingers for a while.

52. A Shooting Star

This day would have been my mother's birthday. No—this day is the day of my mother's birthday. Think of the celebrations and the many anticipations of each birthday. My mother would tell of parties when she was a child with friends and family on the front lawn of her home. Gifts from my family and my brother's family would certainly arrive at the farm each birthday for many years. My mother nearly reached the birthday of her ninety-third year, short by two weeks at the end of April.

I still watch each spring for the first stems of the shooting star. When young, at the time of my mother's birthday, I would gather bouquets of shooting stars at the edge of the woods and take them to her as my offering of love and a celebration of the arrival of spring.

I have placed again on the table beside my bed the tattered leather-covered Bible inscribed to my mother when she was eleven years old: "Alice M. Holloway, 1917, from Mother and Father." There is a cloth bookmark at the beginning of Ecclesiastes. First verse: "The words of the Preacher, the son of David, king of Jerusalem. Vanity of vanities, saith the Preacher, vanity of vanities; all is vanity." What comes from all our labors under the sun? The fourth verse is of some consolation: "One generation passeth away, and another generation cometh: but the earth abideth for ever."

As a child, my mother had taken care to note John 3: 16 on the flyleaf of her Bible and had marked the verse — "For God so loved the world." With the assurance of not perishing, of everlasting life when one believes. The Bible is filled between the pages with clippings saved from printed matter. One is of "beatitudes for friends of the aged." My mother knew, found comfort in, and gave thanks, sitting at night in the farmhouse: "Blessed are they who make it known that I'm loved, respected and not alone." She was waiting for us to come to her that April morning shortly before another celebration of her birthday.

53. Walworth County

What is the first thing that you remember in your life? This will be the event that marks you as a conscious human being and the event that impressed you enough to be committed to memory all these years of your life. This is the event that likely gives you your identity, the primal event that has lasted a lifetime.

For me, it is standing east of the barn with my father and watching an old man slowly making his way across the field from the Old Place. My father tells me that the man is his father. I have no memory of my grandfather before my father said to me that his father was coming across the field to see us. Startled into consciousness, I would remember this forever.

I was then nearing the age of five, and my grandfather was in his seventy-eighth year. I am now nearly his age as he crossed the field for perhaps his last visit to the farm. I do not remember his arrival that day, nor do I remember ever seeing him again. The crossing with recognition of him by my father was everything to me.

My world was the few miles that radiated from the farm to the boundaries of Walworth County. My relatives all lived within a few miles of the farm and each other. The generations before them had settled in the county, and that is where they had lived their lives. Ancestors rest now in the well-kept cemeteries throughout the county.

Each Memorial Day my brother and I place flowers at the gravesites. Most of all, we remember and celebrate our ancestors, and give thanks for the lives that came before us, giving us our lives.

54. Birth Day

My birthday on the sixteenth of May has been gloriously celebrated. Solveig wished me a happy birthday as soon as I woke up. Annie and Bryan and my new grandson, Fyntan, flew up from Memphis for a visit. Laura and Billy and my grandsons Daniel and Julian called in the afternoon, singing me a happy birthday song. My brother, Ralph, and Lois sent me birthday wishes and a reminder to enjoy the moment. We dined with long-time friends Paul and Mari Jo. One candle was lit on the cake, taking me back to my very first birthday when my mother and father placed me at the farmhouse window and photographed me with a cake of one candle as I looked into the new world of possibilities.

Let this be the year—my seventy-seventh—of practicing, unceasingly, loving kindness. *Metta*—the Pali word that is known in Buddhist practice as "loving-kindness"—embraces the connection of all beings, invites calmness and clarity of mind and heart, and fosters a life of compassion. This is the practice that prepares us for the times ahead—especially the sufferings that come with aging and death. But most of all, this is the practice that is integral to a life well lived. My friend Paul Thoresen sent me a metta blessing as a birthday wish.

May you be safe and protected.
May you be healthy in mind, body and spirit.
May you be at peace and at ease.
May you be happy.

My birthday ends this year with a reading of *The Diamond Sutra*. I find solace and relief in a reminder of the impermanence of all things. So much of our suffering comes from the attempt to live with ignorance of impermanence. We spend a lifetime creating things—physical and otherwise—that ultimately must pass away. And, being human, we easily lament the passing and suffer the loss of what we have constructed and known in our lives as our conditioned existence. At the end of the sutra, variously translated from the Sanskrit, the Buddha responds to questions on the nature of the world humanly perceived.

All composed things are like a dream,
a phantom, a drop of dew, a flash of lightning.
That is how to meditate on them.
That is how to observe them.

Thus have I heard.

55. Trolls

And yet we continue to construct illusions that will explain our experiences and give us comfort in their consequences. This is part of our human evolution. This is also the source of much of our suffering, when we seek permanence in all things that are transitory, when we try to find answers in a world of illusion.

Perhaps the ancient—as well as contemporary—Scandinavian tales of the trolls provide relief in the search for rational and scientific explanations. The forces of nature are personified in creatures that play tricks on us night and day. Climb the mountains in Norway, travel into the fjords, hear the thunder and see the lightning, walk through the woods—and you will begin to think about the trolls.

I keep looking at the illustration made by Norwegian artist Birger Moss Johnsen for the folk tale "The Three Billy Goats Gruff" in the collection titled *Eventyr for Barn*. Pictured is the largest of the goats confronting the troll under the bridge. "Who's that tripping over my bridge?" roared the troll. "I'm coming to gobble you up." We know from the tale that the troll will be done away with, and that all three goats will cross the bridge and go into the mountains and eat and become fat. And the story, being Norwegian, will end: "Snip, snap, snout. This tale's told out!"

The Troll

56. Loving Kindness

The Rapture did not come during the weekend as predicted. The date will be reset and expectations will be adjusted. But, isn't the scripture clear in Matthew 24: 42 that the time of the coming is uncertain? "Therefore keep watch, because you do not know what day our Lord will come." At other places in the Bible, including the Book of Revelation, the day of the Lord will come like a thief, like a thief in the night. The coming will catch us by surprise, suddenly, when we least expect it.

Welcome is the realization that the kingdom has already come. Or, precisely, that it comes each day when we are ready and aware, when we are keeping watch for the spiritual to be present in our lives each day here on Earth.

Nothing like pain with the prospect of surgery to bring you to the watch, night and day. On good therapeutic and spiritual advice, I am reading and following the meditation practices in Sharon Salzberg's *Lovingkindness: The Revolutionary Art of Happiness*. I would have my religion be kindness, a religion that fosters calmness, clarity of mind and heart, and compassion and understanding. Love, removing us from fear, is the healing force. "When we feel love," says Salzberg, "our mind is expansive and open enough to include the entirety of life in full awareness, both its pleasures and its pains. We feel neither betrayed by pain nor overcome by it, and thus we can contact that which is undamaged within us regardless of the situation."

A loving heart, we are reminded in *Lovingkindness*, "even for the duration of a snap of a finger, makes one a truly spiritual being." A spiritual life daily is rapture enough, the kingdom come.

57. Memorial Day

It is a cold and wet morning and rain steadily is falling as I drive to the farm. I am meeting Ralph in Whitewater, as he drives down from Ripon. From there we will go to the cemeteries in Tibbets and Delavan to place flowers at the graves of our parents, grandparents, and great-grandparents. The cemeteries are being prepared for the Memorial Day services to be held on Monday.

Ralph does the digging and planting this year as I watch from the cab of the truck. Not long ago my mother waited in the car as I tended to the graves. I hear my brother wondering aloud if the tending of graves will continue, noting that fewer flowers are being seen at the cemetery.

The rain subsides for the day as we drive to the farm to check on the conversion that is taking place. A portion of the farm is being readied for a community supported agricultural operation. The stanchions in the barn have been removed, gutters have been filled with concrete, an enormous cooler has been moved into the north end of the barn, and equipment for the cleaning and processing of vegetables has been installed. The farm has survived and will continue to provide a sustainable agriculture. I celebrate the family that once made this place a home and a family farm.

58. Box Elder

Springtime regeneration is all around us. And within us. Even the old ones find hope and strength to continue on. Since moving to Madison ten years ago, I have walked almost daily up the street a few blocks to the corner that is marked by the aging box elder tree. I have made its portrait several times with my camera. Especially haunting and symbolic is the box elder on spring days as the tree holds on another season for dear life. Visually, the old box elder only improves with age. The outer bark becomes gnarled and scarred, and decay from within makes for dark cavities.

In Donald Culross Peattie's elegantly written *Natural History of North American Trees,* republished now in a single volume, the box elder takes its place among the native species. The box elder was extensively planted at one time in the Midwest to provide quick and cheap effect. Peattie states the conventional view of the tree: "Though it does soon begin to give a respectable amount of shade, it is a short-lived tree; its weak wood, worthless except for fuel, undistinguished in color and grain, all too easily splits when violated by wind and sleet storms; its leaves, in the eastern states, generally turn crisp and brown in fall, without ever assuming any of the beautiful autumnal tints of the Maples." Peattie then praises the virtues of the box elder: "Many people appreciate its resistance to heat, cold, drought, and ceaseless winds that would soon kill species with more exalted reputations. And even in winter it has its charms, with those smooth bright green twigs that bear, so precociously, in early spring the curious flowers." I grew up on the farm with box elders seeding themselves in a hundred different places in field and yard.

Steel woven cables have been wound around the trunk of my box elder here in town. They hold the tree together, extending the life the aging tree. Weeds and grasses circle the base of my box elder. New leaves fill the branches that remain. Certainly I am not the only passerby who receives daily lessons from this proud elder standing on the corner of Anthony Lane and Odana Road.

59. Tonglen Practice

For a long time I have had on my bookshelf, within easy reach, *The Tibetan Book of Living and Dying,* by Sogyal Rinpoche. It presents and clarifies the classic *Tibetan Book of the Dead* and offers meditation practices for Tibetan Buddhism. Twenty years ago, when Sogyal Rinpoche's book was published, I read portions and wrote at the front that I must return to this book "in time of need." In preparation for surgery, I recently asked a counselor for help, and he recommended the book, referring me to the part on the Tibetan practice of Tonglen. I enter here, for the record, the fact that Tonglen is informing much of my thought and spiritual life.

Tonglen in Tibetan means "giving and receiving." It is a practice of opening yourself to the truth of suffering, to the suffering of the self and the suffering of others. Rinpoche writes: "No other practice I know is as effective in destroying the self-grasping, self-cherishing, self-absorption of the ego, which is the root of our suffering and the root of all hard-heartedness."

Evoking compassion in yourself is the beginning of the practice. A range of methods is given, starting with a meditation on loving kindness. "Let your heart open now, and let love flow from it: then extend this love to all beings." Throughout the practice, the movement is toward a compassionate wish to attain enlightenment for the benefit of others. "In the Tonglen practice of giving and receiving, we *take* on, *through compassion,* all the various mental and physical sufferings of all beings: their fear, frustration, pain, anger, guilt, bitterness, doubt, and rage, and we *give* them, *through love,* all our happiness, and well-being, peace of mind, healing, and fulfillment." As I breathe in, I am taking in the suffering of all beings, my own included, and as I breathe out, I am giving love and happiness and well-being.

The practice of Tonglen is known by many names in all the religious and spiritual traditions. A better world, here on Earth, will come with the everyday, noble practice of giving unto others, giving unto others as you would compassionately give unto yourself.

60. And Then What?

I have received from Jerry Rosco, the biographer of Glenway Wescott, a manuscript of the last journals written by Wescott. Jerry had written the introduction to my Borderland Books publication of Wescott's *Goodbye, Wisconsin*. After many years of researching, collecting, and editing the journals, Jerry provides the last entry made by Wescott three years before dying in 1987. It was Memorial Day, and he wrote: "Is it possible that I may fail to ever write again? Again and again in the early morning I take a page of the pink paper that delights me, punched three times for my habitual three-ring binders, and then what?" Wescott valued the craft of writing to the end. Writing daily in the journal was among the last things to go.

Much earlier in his life, when he was in his twenties, Wescott traveled by train from Chicago to the small town in central Wisconsin where his parents were living after retiring from farming at the edge of the Kettle Moraine. He had already been to Europe, living among the expatriate writers, and he was returning for a visit during the Christmas holiday. Wescott described the journey on the train, his days of visiting, and his reflections on Wisconsin and the Midwest, in the introduction to the book he published in 1928 as *Goodbye, Wisconsin*. When I republished the book, I

Train in Wisconsin

commissioned my artist friend Steve Chappell to made a woodblock print of the train speeding through the Wisconsin countryside. The artwork, evoking Wescott's return to Wisconsin and his leaving, graces the cover of the book.

This from Wescott's writing on leaving Wisconsin on the train in the night: "Over many little bridges the train makes a soft thunder. A piece of moon has come up. In front of it a grove of naked trees, a flat expanse of dreary silver tarnished by weed-tops thrusting through it, a broken-looking house, a town, a living but icy river, rapidly give place to each other; as in the foreground of a writer's attention possible subjects for a book vary and shift before that waxing, waning, one-sided radiance which is his own spirit and about which alone he has no choice." Wescott, from a farm in Wisconsin, lived the writer's life for the rest of his life.

I write this now in my treasured three-ring binder. Below my window, this day in early June, the peonies arc blooming gloriously all over the lawn. The shades of red and pink. And then what?

Summer

61. Haiku

Let the summer of 2011 begin with two haiku from *A Chime of Windbells* and *A Net of Fireflies:*

The grasses mown at dawn are carried through
The farmhouse gate: how cool and fresh with dew!
—Bonchô

A sudden downpour! Thunderclouds are cracking!
And round the farmhouse all the ducks run, quacking!
—Kiraku

These because they take me back to the coming of spring at the farm. Time for the first mowing of hay in the field. And thunderstorms that come suddenly with the darkening of sky after a morning of enormous clouds floating in the sky. And in late afternoon the sun will shine again, and we will be treated to a perfect rainbow filling the eastern sky. Someone calls out to watch for the pot of gold.

62. Evening Chores

Hallelujah! The harbinger of a real Midwest summer. Hot and humid air expands north from the south as high pressure builds at all levels of the atmosphere. A combination of heat, humidity, and sunshine will create dangerous conditions. Already over one thousand record highs have been established. Temperatures today climb toward a hundred degrees, and we are warned that humidity will become oppressive. The weather brings us to attention.

And how is the farm boy as he herds the cows in the pasture east of the barn? We keep an eye on him as he rounds up the cows for another evening of chores. He came to mind again last night as I continued my reading of *Falling into Grace* by Adyashanti. The author reminds us, as he recounts his own spiritual development, that "awakening," or "enlightenment," is not a goal to be reached one time only. There is no end point in a spiritual life, but we are always in the process of awakening into another reality. Spiritual awakening comes with the letting go of the self-centeredness of striving for enlightenment. By letting go of the suffering caused by the desire to be enlightened. He writes, "People in the spiritual world are often busy meditating, chanting the name of God, and doing various spiritual practices and prayers as a means of trying to bring happiness to themselves or to garner God's grace. Spiritual people often listen to the teachings of great awakened ones and try to apply them, but they often miss the key element, and that is: We're addicted to being ourselves. We're addicted to our own self-centeredness. We're addicted to our suffering. We're addicted to our beliefs and our worldview. We really think that the universe would collapse if we relinquished our part in it. In this way, we actually want to continue suffering."

Herding the ox, no matter how the stages are conceived and divided, is movement out of the dream world of the mind and into the world of reality. Adyashanti reminds us that awakening comes in the recognition of the unborn. "The invitation is for all of us to stay in beginner's mind, to always stay in touch with the unborn, the undying, and the uncreated, because it's from that potential that something in us awakens that is free from strife and suffering and that has been waiting in every single one of us to express itself." Our lives become "an expression of that which is inexpressible, unexplainable, and indefinable." All is possible in the pasture at the farm.

63. Mabel's Diary

When clearing out the farmhouse, I found in the desk drawer the diary that Mabel Stiles Holloway kept for the year 1939. Mabel married my grandfather Will Holloway in 1924, several years after the death of my grandmother Lorena, my mother's mother. We often visited my grandfather and Mabel, and they came to visit us several times each week. Our family would drive the three miles north to Millard to spend evenings, often joined by Mabel's two sisters and their families. Evenings usually ended with the serving of a cake or pie baked that day by Mabel.

As I read Mabel's diary of 1939, the year that I was five years old, I am placed in a world that I was just beginning to know. And slowly reading the diary, I find myself entering the lives of those now gone. And, in a mysterious way, I have a sense that I am continuing to live their lives. Living their lives as might be understood through quantum physics or spiritual mysticism, or through the biological memory of DNA, or through the good example of how they lived. Our ancestors are with us always.

I am impressed with the great amount of activity that filled the days of my grandfather and Mabel. There were daily trips to towns nearby—Delavan, Elkhorn, Fort Atkinson, Whitewater—and to towns and cities farther away at least once a week—Madison, Janesville, Racine. As clerk of Sugar Creek Township, my grandfather often had business to attend to, taking him and Mabel to various meetings and public events. They visited, or were visited by, relatives almost daily. And there were the trips to doctors and dentists and the shopping trips for food, clothing, and hardware.

This was a community. At random, an entry for November 7: "Tuesday evening. We went to a 4-H banquet at Tibbets. Johnsons and Fosses were there, too. Will was called on to make a few remarks." The next day, November 8: "I helped at Methodist Church in Delavan. They served chicken pie for their annual supper. They had a swell supper. We left about 7:30 P.M. for home and to get ready for another celebration, Paddock's 40th wedding anniversary. Willard and family and Dewey and Lizzie called for us—we took a cake (Sunshine)—each family gave a quarter. They served a nice lunch and had a fine program. I had rather a full day. Furnished one chicken for the Methodist supper."

Recorded is the funeral of my grandfather John Quinney. I note the purchase of "caps for the Quinney boys for their birthdays." My grandfather suffers from hay fever and asthma in the month of September. Thanksgiving Day is celebrated at the home of Mabel's sister and family—the Millers—in Fort Atkinson. At the end of December, Mabel writes that they have received sixty-five Christmas cards. The journal closes: "Goodby Old Year with all your joys and sorrows! We turn our faces toward the dawn of a new Year."

I visited Mabel for the last time in 1961, at the Homestead Convalescent Hospital in Delavan, where she was spending her final days. I had returned from upstate New York where I was beginning my first year of university teaching. Two years earlier, my grandfather had been struck and killed by a speeding car as he was walking home from the Millard grocery store. Gone, the generation of grandparents. Life would have to be lived in other ways.

64. Crossing the Street

The situation has changed. Early in the morning my primary doctor called to tell me that hip surgery—the hip replacement—scheduled for two weeks from now must be canceled. Results from a physical examination last week indicate the need for more tests to determine if I have too many risk factors for the surgery. Appointments are being made with cardiologist, urologist, and neurologist. As my friend Gordon, a doctor, tells me, my case is complex. Again, I am being reminded of the clear and present signs of aging, my aging.

My daughter Laura came for a visit during the weekend. She and I had crossed many streets together before, but this time I was having difficulty walking securely as we were about to cross the street on our way to the car after attending a friend's opening exhibition of photographs. Laura offered me her arm for help—and I had the surprising and spontaneous reaction of wanting to avoid assistance, followed immediately by a mixture of gratitude and acceptance. In the few short steps with my daughter, I was learning something new, and I was becoming more aware of the present reality.

I am reading carefully the passages on the management of pain and suffering in Sharon Salzberg's *Lovingkindness*. She writes: "We are brought up with the feeling that suffering is somehow wrong or to be avoided. We get the idea that suffering is unbearable and should not even be faced." Acknowledging our suffering, and opening to it, is relief from a burden. Awareness of the infirmities now experienced in my life is recognition of what is true. And recognizing the truth, beyond illusion, is the first step in developing compassion. Compassion for myself and compassion for all others.

Without judgment, we see that some things bring pain and others bring happiness. We can learn to act without the effects of aversion. Salzberg writes, "To view life compassionately, we have to look at what is happening and at the conditions that gave rise to it." This life is an expression of what we understand, care about, and value. May the suffering of aging help me to be more compassionate in my daily life.

65. The Wisharts of LaGrange

In the box marked "Unknown" I found a photograph made in the late 1870s that I can now identify as being a portrait of my great-great-grandparents James and Joyce Wishart. The Wisharts emigrated from England in 1828, settling in Clinton, New York, and moved by boat and wagon to LaGrange, Wisconsin, in 1844. Their youngest child, Ellen, would later marry Charles Taylor, and Charles and Ellen would give birth to Lorena, who would marry Will Holloway and give birth to my mother.

James and Joyce Wishart were accompanied to LaGrange by John Wishart, the Scottish father of James, and his Scottish wife, Ann Stockdale. Descendants to this day note the martyrdom of George Wishart, who was burned at the stake by the Catholic Church for heresy in Saint Andrews, Scotland, in 1546, and honorably claim him as an ancestor.

James had apprenticed to the trade of blacksmithing before emigrating. He continued to be a blacksmith in LaGrange, as well as a farmer, until he died in 1882. Joyce died two years earlier. They were the parents of eight surviving children. In the portrait near the end of their pioneering lives, James holds a family Bible.

Among my mother's books was a signed copy of *The Blacksmith's Daughter,* by Cecile Houghton Stury, granddaughter of James and Joyce. Much can be learned about the lives of the LaGrange pioneers from the stories that James and Joyce's daughter Elizabeth passed on to her daughter Cecile. I pay particular attention to the fact that some of the blacksmithing of James was the shoeing of oxen. A team of oxen was highly valued on the prairie at the edge of the Kettle Moraine. I imagine James in his blacksmith shop sharpening plow points, with sparks flying from the anvil as the hammer struck, and nailing the shoes to the hooves of the ox. "Father keeps all the records in a big book of what men owe him and when he collects all of it we will have our home paid for. Nobody can make us move." I have heard from a descendant that he found the ledger in a trunk stored in a shed on the farm of a child of James and Joyce who moved from LaGrange when young to homestead in Mapleton, Minnesota.

We realize, finally, in the allegory of ox herding, that the ox was never lost. How could the ox be lost when our true nature was there from the beginning? All things are an intimate part of the entire cosmos. Nothing needs to be sought; nothing needs to be gained. The treasure is already here, within us and related to everything else, and always changing.

66. Equanimity

Aversion to physical deterioration is a hindrance, in the Buddhist sense, to the lessening of suffering. Readily coming to mind throughout the day, as I take another painful step and as I receive another call from the clinic or the hospital for another medical test, is the thought that this should not be happening to me and that once I was not in this condition, that things should be otherwise. I spend energies trying to push away—to avert—what is really happening. But this I also know: pain and suffering can be alleviated when I can see things as they are, when I recognize impermanence and the changing nature of everything, when I see the constant flow of events that are outside my control, when I cease to make judgments about the way things are. In other words, when I relax to the wise and compassionate state of being known as *equanimity*.

Equanimity, imagined visually, is when the oxherd in the allegory achieves harmony with the ox that is being herded. Imagine the boy in the pasture at the farm walking home in harmony with the cow. Life is in balance.

With the gift of equanimity, as Salzberg notes in her book, suffering can be accepted without aversion: "Thanks to the gift of equanimity, we can develop the courage to stay open to suffering. We can face pain again and again without being overcome by sorrow and misery, without becoming so embittered by them that we have to strike out at them and push them away." In the daily practice of equanimity, one can be at home with things as they are.

Postscript: On some days, and often on the same day that I am one with the ox, I am also at one with Dylan Thomas's cry into the abyss:

> Do not go gentle into that good night,
> Old age should burn and rave at close of day;
> Rage, rage against the dying of the light.

This, as well, is the way things really are. Such is the complex nature of being human and mortal.

67. Roy Chapman Andrews

Sometimes, still, I wake in the morning from dreaming that I am young and ready to begin a great adventure. Sometimes I am contemplating what direction my life could take, what my occupation in life might be. I still have a sense that I am waiting to be called.

One of my earliest inspirations came from reading the autobiography of the explorer and paleontologist Roy Chapman Andrews. I was a freshman in high school in Delavan, in 1948, and I had been browsing in Abrams Public Library in town, before driving home for evening chores. I took from the shelf the book with the brown and yellow jacket that pictured a camel caravan crossing the Gobi Desert. The book was titled *Under a Lucky Star.* I learned immediately that the author was born and grew up just a few miles away, in Beloit. If a boy from Wisconsin, from my part of Wisconsin, could become an explorer and discoverer of dinosaur eggs in the Gobi Desert, what might be possible for me?

After a childhood of exploring the natural world along the Rock River and in the woods and fields of southern Wisconsin, Andrews attended Beloit College. After graduation he traveled to New York and asked for a job at the American Museum of Natural History, where he started as a sweeper of floors and eventually became a naturalist, explorer, and director of the

Roy Chapman Andrews

museum. Andrews led a series of daring journeys, known as the Central Asiatic Expeditions, into uncharted expanses of Mongolia, and unearthed a treasure-trove of fossils of dinosaurs and many species of extinct reptiles and mammals. The expeditions constituted one of the most innovative episodes in the annals of scientific discovery.

In memory of Roy Chapman Andrews, and in recognition of the importance of the book in my own life, I republished *Under a Lucky Star* as one of my Borderland Books. My friend Steve Chappell made sketches for the book. Andrews's reflection about his own calling would be printed on the jacket of the book: "From the time that I can remember anything I always intended to be an explorer, to work in a natural history museum, and to live out of doors. Actually, I never had any choice of profession. I wanted to be an explorer and naturalist so passionately that anything else as a life work just never entered my mind."

Andrews, always the explorer, maintained a sense of wonderment throughout his life. He has been an inspiration to me throughout my life, and continues to be a source for embracing the adventures of life.

68. Once Upon as Island

Once upon a time, on the island, I walked the streets and byways of Manhattan, camera in hand, seeing things I had never seen before. Earlier this year I published the book of photographs from that time and place in my life. At the beginning of the book, I used as an epigraph lines from Walt Whitman's *Leaves of Grass*.

> The question, O me! so sad, recurring—What good
> amid these, O me, O life?
> *Answer.*
> That you are here—that life exists and identity,
> That the powerful play goes on, and you may
> contribute a verse.

For over thirty years I kept the photographs I had taken on the island as the decade of the sixties was ending. As I moved from one place to another, the sleeves of negatives and the trays of slides moved with me, from one closet to another. Someday, I thought, the documentation might serve some unforeseen purpose. If nothing else, the photographs would show the passing of time and the changing of the landscape. I did not know, until September 11, 2001, that the photographs would take on a meaning and significance beyond anything I could have imagined. Always, as with all photographs, we know that their use and meaning will eventually go beyond anything we can now imagine. Photographs are a reminder of the impermanence of all things.

I thought then that I was living at the center of the world. I was part of the movements of the 1960s— civil rights, antiwar protest, counterculture, the war on poverty, avant-garde theater, and pop and radical art. Construction of the World Trade Center was taking place in the dynamic social and political context of the times. Lyndon Johnson had been elected president in 1964 to deliver the programs of the Great Society and to solve—or at least improve upon—the nation's problems of poverty, inequality, education, and urban decay. Yet the escalation of U.S. military intervention in Southeast Asia—half a million troops in Vietnam by the end of 1967—caused cutbacks to domestic programs. Opposition to the war increased, and there were protest marches down Fifth Avenue and bus rides to Washington for huge antiwar demonstrations.

At New York University, where I was teaching, we were questioning not only the war, but also the role of the university. In Washington Square and in the East Village, along First Avenue and Second Avenue and in Tompkins Square Park, another form of resistance was taking place. Hippies and flower children, as the media called them, were on the streets and in the lofts. Abbie Hoffman came to my sociology class, and *Hair* opened at the Public Theater. We were shocked and shaken by the assassinations of Martin Luther King Jr. and Robert Kennedy. Exhausted by the protests against his Vietnam policies, President Johnson announced that he would not run for reelection, and in January of 1969 Richard Nixon was inaugurated as president.

I began to photograph in ways I had never photographed before. I was instructed and inspired by the photographers collectively known as the concerned photographers. I took courses with Sandra Weiner and Cornell Capa, and I met other photographers who were exploring the new cultural landscape. For two years, my last two years in New York, I photographed almost daily what I was seeing and experiencing. Usually I used black and white film in a 35 mm camera. For several months, with color slide film in my camera, I walked to Lower Manhattan and photographed the construction of the World Trade Center. The opposing and conflicting dynamics of the times, as the sixties were ending, could be seen as one world was coming down and another was going up.

As I walked with my camera along the streets of Lower Manhattan, at the construction site, I observed the times in a microcosm. My self-proclaimed project as a sociologist and photographer was to document the changes that were taking place. The public had not generally endorsed the building of the World Trade Center.

Many regarded the project as the triumph of corporate business over the public interest. Local merchants were losing their shops and the neighborhood was vanishing, bulldozed to make way for corporate headquarters. The police heavily patrolled the area. Construction workers boldly displayed the American flag, and protesters of the war and the construction were present daily.

There was excitement and fascination with the construction of this major building project by the employees on Wall Street, by nearby residents, by visitors to the city, and by much of the population of Manhattan. The sounds were of jackhammers and pile drivers, the constant grind and roar of heavy equipment, and the voices of the workers. And there were the moments of repose, workers lunching and taking breaks, talking to each other. Men and women stood quietly and viewed the site. Vendors sold their wares from the street. And there was the photographer—inspired—releasing the shutter of the camera with great joy. With hopes of contributing a verse to the great play that was going on.

69. Ensō

An integral part of the Zen world is the tradition of ensō drawing and painting. The word *ensō* means "circle," and the drawing or painting of the circle symbolizes wholeness, enlightenment, the cosmos, the absolute of everything and the void of nothingness. The aesthetic of ensō, as minimalist expressionist art, is immersion in the present moment. The ensō, for me, is the boy coming home with the ox at the end of the day.

In Zen Buddhist art, the ensō represents a moment of freedom in the creation of the artwork. Traditionally, the brushed ink is done on silk or rice paper in one movement of the brush. The spirit of the artist is expressed in that one moment. Some artists draw daily the ensō as a spiritual practice.

My friend Carol Chase Bjerke is inspired by the ensō and has been using the form in her own art. This year Carol has been drawing ensō circles on photographic paper, then developing and printing the images. We both have learned much in our meditations on the ensō. Circles of wholeness, new beginnings, and being here now.

Ensō

70. Not to Be Forgotten

Not to be forgotten, as the arc of the summer sun already begins to lower, are the later days of our voyager, Odysseus. He is still wandering, roving through the towns, oar on his shoulder, with thoughts of the journey home. Knowing the words of the prophet, he speaks of ripe old age and what must be.

> And at last my own death will steal upon me…
> A gentle, painless death, far from the sea it comes
> To take me down, borne down with the years in ripe
> old age
> With all my people here in blessed peace around me.
> All this, the prophet said, will come to pass.

His wife, Penelope, hopes for a happy old age.

In the meantime, not to be forgotten, in spite of what will come to pass, or because of what will come to pass, is the understanding of our true home. Astronomically, everything in the universe is moving away from everything else. There is no fixed reference point in the universe that we can call home. Every point, then, is home. We are at home everywhere.

We are an intimate part of everything, of the great evolving whole, rather than separate and isolated individuals without a home. We abide everywhere, aware that our ultimate existence is beyond this body that we know existentially as our own. I read again, as reminder, the paragraph from Salzberg's *Lovingkindess:* "When we identify with the body as a separate self, as our only home, we think we must control it in order to preserve our sense of who we are. But we cannot control sickness or old age or death. If we try, we bear the inevitable burdens of hopelessness and powerlessness. When we conceive ourselves as finite and separate, how fearful death becomes!"

We—our minds and our bodies—are joined in all of the matter, energy, and spirit of the universe, and of the matter, energy, and spirit of the universes beyond. Each breath we take, each breath we make, is a joining with everything that is beyond the self that we narrowly conceive as distinct and separate, permanent and unchanging.

A morning message from artist friend Russell Gardner tells me that he had breakfast with a friend and asked him what he means by "spiritual." His friend, a man of considerable age, answered, "I think of its root: to inspire, as in breathing." Just the breathing, that we are here, that we exist, and that we are breathing to keep alive. No other visions, miracles, rituals, or doctrines are needed this day.

71. Gerald Gregg

I found a drawing several years ago that a relative has since identified as the work of my cousin Gerald Gregg. Gerald was born in 1907 and lived most of his life in Racine. I remember being in his company as a child when we would visit the home of his parents, Myra and Tom. Gerald's grandmother, from the Bray family, and my great-grandmother were sisters. Gerald had completely and permanently lost his hearing from a childhood infection. I would be spellbound as he signed with his mother and his wife on the sofa in the Racine house.

During the Depression, after graduating from the Layton School of Art in Milwaukee, Gerald found freelance assignments. In 1935, the Western Printing and Lithographing Company hired him to do the covers for Dell paperbacks. He also drew Disney and Warner Brothers comic strips and all the back covers for the series of Little Golden Books. Books with sensational graphic covers, including Agatha Christie's *Boomerang Clue,* Gaston Leroux's *Phantom of the Opera,* Dashiell Hammett's *A Man Called Spade,* and H. G. Wells's *Invisible Man.*

Gerald worked with airbrush, and it was his unique technique that made the covers, a stylized realism, the classics that they are today. In addition to his airbrush work, he produced paintings in oils and watercolors, and pen-and-ink drawings. Original paintings occasionally appear for sale on the art market.

I study daily the ink sketch, with watercolors, of the thatched cottage with the picket fence partially appearing in the foreground. Happy knowing that we have an artist—this artist—in our family.

72. In This World

Extreme heat continues through the week in the heartland. Temperatures of one hundred–plus degrees are combined with high humidity and sunshine. There are warnings to drink plenty of water, wear light-colored clothing, and avoid strenuous activity. I'm finally having air-conditioning installed in the living room. And I fear for those endangered by the heat in sweltering rooms.

From across the room, Van Morrison is singing his stream of consciousness song "Madame George." A spiritual sense of desire and loss and remembrance of things past.

> That's when you fall
> When you fall into a trance
> Sitting on a sofa playing games of chance
> With your folded arms in history books you glance
> Into the eyes of Madame George.

Say good-bye to Madame George and dry your eyes for Madame George and wonder why for Madame George. "Get on the train, get on the train."

The Dalai Lama tells an audience in Chicago that everyone wants a happy life. That happiness begins with honesty, which creates trust, which leads to friendship, which means happiness. Religion has nothing to do with it, he tells the audience, adding that moral principles are not rooted in religious doctrine but in the pursuit of happiness. It all comes down to happiness.

The media empire of Rupert Murdoch is shaken by the scandal of phone hacking as he appears before a committee of the British Parliament. The crisis over the extension of debt limits in the United States, debated by Republicans and Democrats, is nearing the default deadline. The spacecraft *Atlantis,* in its last flight, is on its way back to Earth. There is a change of generals in the Afghan War. Severe draught and famine are taking place in Somalia. In this reality of nature and world of our making, what center is there to hold on to? My heavy head spins at once with the universe. The Indian guru in Somerset Maugham's novel *The Razor's Edge* speaks of the infinite goodness of the universe, of which we are inevitably part and parcel.

It is to the book we turn, repeatedly, for a grounding of mind and body and spirit. This is another way of returning to the herding of the ox, to walking peacefully in happiness with the ox that was thought to be missing. That book, for today, is *Falling into Grace* by the Zen master known as Adyashanti. Near the end of the book Adyashanti reminds us that it is vitally important that we understand that we regularly inhabit two different worlds.

One world, the one we humans are born into, is the world of opposites, the world of relativity. A world composed of good and bad, of love and hate, of should and should not, distinctions that make sense for living in the world we humans have created. This is the conventional world we live in most of the time.

But there is another world, a whole other state of consciousness that is beyond the world of duality, beyond the relativity of conventional human existence. This other world, Adyashanti reminds us, is what Jesus referred to as "the kingdom of Heaven." This is what the Buddha called nirvana—life lived outside the realm of relativity, outside the ego of conventional consciousness.

We cannot live without being a part of the conventional, dualistic world. We have to function in the relative world in order to survive. But with an awareness of mind we can, as various Buddhist masters have instructed, "abide in non-abiding." We can, following the words of Jesus, be "in this world, but not of it." We can live in both the world of relativity and the world of ultimate reality. Our human existence includes the relative, but it is not entirely defined by relative reality. Adyashanti writes this about the consciousness of living in both worlds simultaneously: "This state of consciousness is the hardest place to describe, because it is literally indescribable. The highest reality is being both 'this' and 'that' and neither; being both spirit and human; being a field of open, spacious awareness, as well as one particular human incarnation. This is something that takes great subtlety, a deep willingness to go beyond all of our notions, even our notions of good and bad, and right and wrong."

A letting go, a surrendering, to the search and quest for spiritual enlightenment. The ox was never missing; the divine is always present. From *Falling into Grace:* "When we look out the window, there's a tree, a garbage can, the grass, a flower, a human being. All of this is actually the face of God. Look in the mirror; that's what God looks like today. Look out the window; that's your true self. That's your true nature being manifest at this moment." No place to go, nothing to run away from, because there is nowhere to go. "Here is the only place there is."

The gift of wholeness. An openness of heart and mind. My prayer is a letting go, an opening of myself to the entire cosmos.

73. We Gather Together

For several years I have been working on the poem I call "We Gather Together." It is a poem to be recited aloud by those gathered together on various occasions of joy and of sorrow.

We who dwell on a vast continent
That stretches into the universe
Gather together.

In times of joy and times of sorrow,
In the changing of the seasons,
We gather together

To care for one another,
To live our lives with purpose,
To find wisdom, compassion, and strength,
And to know the oneness of all things.

Let us listen.
Let us follow the rhythm of life's mystery
And join in its dance.

Formed each moment by the way we live,
We give thanks
For this life together.

74. A Postcard

You look at the canvas—the one by Georges-Pierre Seurat—the painting titled *Sunday Afternoon on the Island of La Grande Jatte,* completed in 1886. Your eye optically connects the dots of paint to make new colors. I have done this several times on my visits to the Art Institute of Chicago.

This week I have been watching on DVD *Sunday in the Park with George* by Stephen Sondheim and James Lapine, the musical that explores the Seurat painting. The figures in the painting come to life, their stories are told, and the life of the painter is examined. A dedicated artist, Seurat did not always connect the dots in his own life, held relationships at a distance. But on canvas, from the blank canvas, he painted and created images of beauty. I watch and listen again and again to Sondheim's song "Finishing the Hat." Seurat, played by Mandy Patinkin, stands at the window in Paris watching the rest of the world, and paints. "Mapping out a sky." "What you feel like, planning a sky." "Studying the hat." "Stepping back to look at a face." "There's a part of you always standing by." "Finishing a hat." And the lines of epiphany at the end of the song: "Look, I made a hat.../Where there never was a hat."

My daughter Laura and her family are in Paris. Laura sends me photos from her cell phone of the places I used to take her when visiting Paris forty-some years ago. I watched, long ago, as she played for whole afternoons in the Luxembourg Gardens. To my grandsons, as they prepared for their first trip to Paris, I sent the words from the ending of Ernest Hemingway's *A Moveable Feast*. Each time that I have gone to Paris I have read these lines and copied them into my travel journal: "There is never any ending to Paris and the memory of each person who has lived in it differs from that of any other. We always returned to it no matter who we were or how it was changed or with what difficulties, or ease, it could be reached. Paris was always worth it and you received return for whatever you brought to it."

I have found in one of Kate's albums a picture postcard sent to her from Paris in the summer of 1906. Kate, my grandfather Quinney's sister, was working in Chicago then as a seamstress and hat maker. She made fine hats for the wealthy society women of Chicago, from materials purchased at Marshall Field. The postcard is from "Inga," one of the women who would be wearing a hat made by Kate. On the front of the postcard, she wrote that Paris is "a very gay place," and that she is having a nice time. Kate never went to Paris. When she retired she returned to the house on the farm at the Old Place.

75. Prepare a Ship

Many times over the course of this year I have thought of D. H. Lawrence. Of his life, his novels, short stories, and travel writings, and his poems. I knew that I must eventually write a few words in my journal about Lawrence. He suffered from tuberculosis much of his life, moved from one residence to another, and died in 1930. His life and work are documented in John Worthen's *D. H. Lawrence: The Life of an Outsider.* Earlier this year I purchased a copy of Lawrence's *Last Poems,* published posthumously. His religious poem "The Ship of Death" was being written as he lay dying.

The last poems were influenced by his exploration and study of Etruscan tombs in Italy. Lawrence wrote: "To the Etruscan all was alive; the whole universe lived; and the business of man was himself to live amid it all. He had to draw life into himself, out of the wandering huge vitalities of the world. The cosmos was alive, like a vast creature." The force could be known as God, or as the gods, and as the soul of our being.

Lawrence leads us into the underworld of mythology. He tells us that in the Etruscan tombs he saw "the sacred treasures of the dead, the little bronze ship of death that should bear him over to the other world, the vases of jewels for his arraying, the vases of small dishes, the little bronze statuettes and tools, the armour."

The "little bronze ship of death" is the central image in Lawrence's last poem, "The Ship of Death." Fragments of the poem:

> Have you built your ship of death, O have you?
> O build your ship of death, for you will need it.
>
> Oh build your ship of death, your little ark
> and furnish it with food, with little cakes, and wine
> for the dark flight to oblivion.

And at the end of the poem is a vision of resurrection:

> The flood subsides, and the body, like a worn sea-shell
> emerges strange and lovely.
> And the little ship wings home, faltering and lapsing on
> the pink flood,
> and the frail soul steps out, into her house again
> filling the heart with peace.

You are left with wonder and reverence. Still not knowing, but at peace. This is the voyage that awaits us all.

76. Swallowtails in August

Two large swallowtail butterflies fly daily from bush to bush and flower to flower on the lawn. Resident butterflies—much welcomed—for the month of August. I watch for long periods of time from a chair on the balcony. These swallowtails, in all their beauty, are already in the fourth stage of a swallowtail's cycle of life.

Many of the ideas and thoughts that first come to us in words—in conversations with others and in our solitary reading—become integral to our being. A word that I have remembered for years, and have tried to incorporate into my life, is *inter-being,* which Vietnamese Buddhist master Thich Nhat Hanh uses in his writings and teaching. Nothing exists by itself alone; everything depends on every other thing. From this perspective, all being is inter-being.

Impermanence, no separate self, and inter-being are represented in the example of the flower. In Hanh's words in his book *No Death, No Fear:* "We can describe the flower as being full of everything. There is nothing that is not present in the flower. We see sunshine, we see the rain, we see clouds, we see the earth, and we also see time and space in the flower. A flower, like everything else, is made entirely of non-flower elements. The whole cosmos has come together in order to help the flower manifest herself. The flower is full of everything except one thing: a separate self, a separate identity."

On this piece of paper on which I write, we can ask: "Piece of paper, where do you come from?" And the same can be asked about the one who writes on this paper. I am everything that makes what I imagine as being me, myself, a self that is everything else. Impermanent and always changing, transforming into something else.

With the understanding of inter-being, of our connection to everything else, without a separate existence, the enlightened person is compassionate and engages in actions to relieve the suffering of others. The *bodhisattva*—the awakened being—helps others to become awakened, as well as being compassionate in their own suffering. The oxherd, in becoming awakened in the course of herding, takes good care of all others. In Buddhist practice, caring for others and their suffering, as you care for yourself and your own suffering, is the vow of the bodhisattva.

The swallowtail butterfly in its life cycle changes from egg to caterpillar to chrysalis to the adult butterfly that is giving me such pleasure this summer. In the process we call metamorphosis, the fully formed swallowtail emerges from the pupal case, finds nourishment in the garden, mates with another swallowtail, and lays eggs in the vegetation. Before summer ends, the caterpillar that emerges from the egg will feed and shed its skin several times as it grows. The caterpillar will find a safe place for the creation of the wondrous chrysalis, from which one day a swallowtail will emerge, drying its moistness in the sun, and taking flight. Is this a new swallowtail butterfly? It is a butterfly from continuous transformation. A metamorphosis. There is no death.

Found among the books in the attic of the farmhouse were a few pages from a book of my childhood, *The Three Little Pigs*. All that remained was the middle section of the book, but enough to bring the memory of the story and its importance to me.

The three little pigs, at the beginning of the book, have sorrowfully left home to seek their livelihoods. The first little pig has met a man with bundles of straw, has been given straw, and has built his house of straw. The wolf has come along, blown the house in with a huff and a puff, and eaten the little pig. This after the little pig said that he would not let the wolf come into the house. "No, no! Not by the hair of my chinny chin chin."

The second little pig has met a man with a bundle of sticks, has been given the sticks, has built his house, and has met the same fate as the first little pig. At this point, in the pages found in the attic, the third little pig meets a man with a wheelbarrow full of bricks and he is given some bricks. He carefully builds his house of bricks and declares that his future is made.

The wolf comes to the brick house. He tells the third little pig that he will huff and puff and blow the house in. And as you know from your own childhood, the wolf cannot blow the brick house in. The wolf then contrives a series of schemes to lure the third little pig out of his house so that he can eat him. First, they are to meet at the turnip patch, but the little pig outsmarts the wolf by going earlier than arranged. Similarly, the little pig goes earlier than arranged to pick apples at Merry Garden. On the last page of the fragment from the attic, the third little pig arrives early at the fair at Shanklin. The illustration shows the pig happily riding on the merry-go-round, waving his cap to fellow fairgoers enjoying their afternoon at the fair.

You will remember the rest of the story: The little pig rolls home in a butter churn to escape the wolf. The wolf goes back to the brick house, very angry indeed, and climbs down the chimney with hopes of eating the third little pig. The pig quickly heats a pot of water in the fireplace. He takes off the cover of the pot as the wolf slides down the chimney and falls into the boiling water. The pig covers the pot, cooks the wolf, and eats him for supper. And we are assured at the end of the story that the little pig lives happily ever afterward.

The classic tale of the three little pigs is older than the first printed version, which appeared in mid-nineteenth-century England. In later versions, the first two pigs escape to the brick house of the third pig, and the wolf is merely singed in the pot and runs away. The moral remains the same: build a sturdy house of bricks and be resourceful when facing the dangers that come your way.

Little Pig at the Fair

But, for me, more immediate and tangible was the fact that pigs played an important part in my early life. My grandfather Will Holloway introduced me to Duroc hogs. He had raised purebred Duroc Jersey hogs on his farm north of Millard—"Wayside Oak Farm." I raised purebred Duroc hogs until I went to college. At the end of each summer, I would show Durocs at the Walworth County Fair. My Durocs were raised for the perpetuation of pigs in the world. And the sale of my purebred Duroc hogs helped to finance my college education.

But more, there was the fair itself at the end of summer. The unstated attraction of the county fair was being able to be away from home for several days after a summer of working in the fields. I spent the nights sleeping in a big tent with other 4-H members. During the day, I would roam the fairgrounds unattended and uninhibited. It was a time to greet neighbors on new territory. My grandfather would be in the Agriculture Building looking at the prize seed corn and the vegetables. Farmers walked around and sat on the latest improvements in machinery. Neighbors picnicked on the green, listening to the band. Others viewed horse races and special acts from the grandstand. I would stop often to listen to country music being played in the radio station tent.

In the imagination, there was something always darkly exotic about the carnival at the fair. It was a source of magic and mystery. I looked forward each year to being caught up in the sounds, vibrant colors, and crowds of the carnival. On the midway, I would see carnival men and women beckoning: a woman offering darts for popping balloons; a man with tattooed arms and an open shirt holding out three balls to knock down a stack of wooden milk bottles. Walking past a tent with an arcade of machines, I would hear loud noises and see people wandering out with cards dispensed from machines for a penny. Other sights would draw me on: motorcycles roaring inside a rickety-walled inverted dome; revolving wooden animals and dragons painted orange, teal, and red; an octopus-shaped ride ablaze with colored lights reaching up and out into the night sky. Once was the summer that I finally sat at the top of the Ferris wheel with the girl of my dreams.

For a lifetime, these summers have marked the end of one season and the beginning of another. Each season invites a new adventure. As a ship sailing from one shore to another.

78. Explorers

How many times have I returned to the last lines of T. S. Eliot's poem "East Coker" from the *Four Quartets?* I read carefully each line and recognize the deep relevance to my own life. The world becomes stranger, the pattern more complicated, and a lifetime burns in every moment. A time for the evening under lamplight.

> Home is where one starts from. As we grow older
> The world becomes stranger, the pattern more
>   complicated
> Of dead and living. Not the intense moment
> Isolated, with no before and after,
> But a lifetime burning in every moment.
> And not the lifetime of one man only
> But of old stones that cannot be deciphered.
> There is a time for the evening under starlight,
> A time for the evening under lamplight
> (The evening with the photograph album).

We, with good fortune, become explorers. The poem continues. Still, and still moving, to a deeper communion with that which is beyond our knowing.

> Love is most nearly itself
> When here and now cease to matter.

Old men ought to be explorers
Here or there does not matter
We must be still and still moving
Into another intensity
For a further union, a deeper communion
Through the dark cold and the empty desolation,
The wave cry, the wind cry, the vast waters
Of the petrel and the porpoise. In my end is my beginning.

The possibility is for a new beginning. Where we began — at home.

79. The Harvest Moon

The Harvest Moon, the legendary full moon that is closest to the autumn equinox and to us, is rising in the eastern sky. Farmers used to harvest crops by the light of this the brightest of moons. We gaze this evening at the moon as it shines in the evening sky.

Shine on, shine on, Harvest Moon, up in the sky. For us all to see. Evening under moonlight, evening under lamplight, a time for the evening at home.

Here, still, ox herding in Wisconsin. I pray the Lord my soul to keep.

Bibliography

Adyashanti. *Falling into Grace*. Boulder, CO: Sounds True, 2011.

Asbjørnsen, P. C., and Jørgen, Moe. *Eventyr for Barn*. Oslo: N. W. Damm & Son, 1963.

Auden, W. H. *For the Time Being*. New York: Random House, 1944.

Bakewell, Sarah. *How to Live*. New York: Other Press, 2010.

Bjerke, Carol Chase. *Hidden Agenda*. Madison, WI: Borderland Books.

Chah, Achaan. *A Still Forest Pool*. Edited by Jack Kornfield and Paul Breiter. Wheaton, IL: Quest Books, 2004.

The Diamond Sutra. Santa Barbara, CA: Concord Grove Press, 1983.

De Maistre, Xavier. *A Journey around My Room* and *A Nocturnal Expedition around My Room*. Translated by Andrew Brown. London: Hesperus Classics, 2004.

Fitzgerald, F. Scott. *The Great Gatsby*. New York: Scribners 1996.

Flesch, William. *British Poetry: 19th Century*. New York: Facts on File, 2010.

Greenough, Sarah. *Harry Callahan*. Boston: Bulfinch Press, 1996.

Hanh, Thich Nhat. *The Diamond That Cuts Through Illusion*. Berkeley, CA: Parallax Press, 2010.

Hanh, Thich Nhat. *No Death, No Fear*. New York: Riverhead Books, 2002.

Homer. *The Odyssey*. Translated by Robert Fagles. New York: Viking Penguin, 1996.

Kornfield, Jack, ed. *The Buddha Is Still Teaching: Contemporary Buddhist Wisdom*. Boston: Shambhala, 2010.

Kwong, Jakusho. *No Beginning, No End: The Intimate Heart of Zen*. Boston: Shambhala, 2010.

LaGrange Pioneers. Walworth County, WI: LaGrange Ladies' Aid Society, 1935.

Lawrence, D. H. *Complete Poems*. New York: Penguin Books, 1993.

Lawrence, D. H. *Last Poems*. Edited by Richard Aldington and Giuseppe Orioli. New York: Viking Press, 1933.

Lunge-Larsen, Lise, and Betsy Bowen. *The Troll with No Heart in His Body*. Boston: Houghton Mifflin, 1999.

Muir, John. *A Thousand-Mile Walk to the Gulf*. Edited by William Frederic Badè. Boston: Houghton Mifflin, 1998.

Peattie, Donald Culross. *The Natural History of North American Trees*. Boston: Houghton Mifflin, 2007.

Quinney, Laura. *William Blake on Self and Soul*. Cambridge, MA: Harvard University Press, 2009.

Rinpoche, Sogyal. *The Tibetan Book of Living and Dying*. San Francisco: Harper San Francisco, 1992.

Ryōkan. *One Robe, One Bowl: The Zen Poetry of Ryōkan*. Trans. and intro. John Stevens. New York: Weatherhill, 1977.

Salzberg, Sharon. *Lovingkindness: The Revolutionary Art of Happiness*. Boston: Shambhala, 1995.

Seo, Audrey Yoshiko. *Ensō: Zen Circles of Enlightenment*. Boston: Weatherhill, 2007.

Stewart, Harold, trans. with essay. *A Chime of Windbells: A Year of Japanese Haiku in English Verse*. Rutland, VT: Charles E. Tuttle, 1969.

Stewart, Harold, trans. with essay. *A Net of Fireflies: Japanese Haiku and Haiku Paintings*. Rutland, VT: Charles E. Tuttle, 1960.

Stury, Cecile Houghton. *The Blacksmith's Daughter*. Dallas, TX: Triangle, 1961.

Thoreau, Henry David. *Walden*. Edited by J. Lyndon Shanley. Princeton, NJ: Princeton University Press, 1973.

Travis, David. *Edward Weston: The Last Years in Carmel*. Chicago: Art Institute of Chicago, 2001.

Wada, Stephanie. *The Oxherder: A Zen Parable Illustrated.* New York: George Braziller, 2002.

Waddell, Norman, trans. with introduction. *The Life and Teaching of Zen Master Bankei.* San Francisco: North Point Press, 1984.

Worster, Donald. *A Passion for Nature: The Life of John Muir.* New York: Oxford University Press, 2008.

Worthen, John. *D. H. Lawrence: The Life of an Outsider.* New York: Counterpoint. 2005.

About the Author

Richard Quinney is author of several books that combine autobiographical writing and photography, including *Journey to a Far Place, For the Time Being, Borderland, Once Again the Wonder, Where Yet the Sweet Birds Sing, Of Time and Place, Field Notes, A Lifetime Burning, Once Upon an Island,* and *A Farm in Wisconsin.* His other books are in the field of sociology. His retrospective book of photographs, *Things Once Seen,* received the August Derleth Award from the Council for Wisconsin Writers. He lives in Madison, Wisconsin.